"If you took an exceptionally talented marketer and had them obsess about personal injury marketing for a decade, they might write a book as useful to law firm owners as this one...but I wouldn't count on it."

—JAMES HELM, TopDog Law

"Rarely in our current world of impersonal relationships do you find a focused, truly sincere, and knowledgeable marketer like Chris Dreyer. Chris is smart and has an excellent moral compass. Simply put, he knows personal injury marketing and is a pleasure to work with. I have learned a lot from Chris both personally and professionally. Most people take. Chris is a giver and his character shows it!"

—HARLAN SCHILLINGER, Legal Marketing Expert

"Chris has talked to and gained knowledge from anyone who's anyone in the personal injury marketing space. On top of that, Chris openly shares all he's learned with others. He's had the meetings, done the interviews, studied the plays—and he has his finger on the pulse of the industry, both where it's been and where it's going."

—DAN MORGAN, Morgan & Morgan

PERSONAL INJURY LAWYER MARKETING

FROM GOOD TO GOAT.

CHRIS DREYER

PIM

**PERSONAL
INJURY
MASTERMIND**

PERSONAL INJURY LAWYER MARKETING
From Good to GOAT
First Edition

ISBN   979-8-9913476-2-4   *Hardcover*
         979-8-9913476-1-7   *Paperback*
         979-8-9913476-0-0   *Ebook*
         979-8-9913476-3-1   *Audiobook*

For Dad:

"*You only play the game to win.*"
—Greg Dreyer

CONTENTS

DISCLAIMER

Look, I'm not an attorney—*you* are. This book is about marketing and advertising. While I won't knowingly say anything that goes against state bar regulations or advertising ethics, you'll still need to make sure that you are aware of your specific guidelines and restrictions before applying any of the advice you read here.

INTRODUCTION

"Fear of rejection, fear of failure holds lawyers
back from doing extraordinary things."

−MIKE PAPANTONIO OF LEVIN PAPANTONIO
Personal Injury Mastermind podcast episode 80

Owning a personal injury law firm is not like *Field of Dreams*—
just because you build it does not mean they will come. You have
to proactively market yourself in order to generate business.

Marketing, like many things in life and business, comes
down to both quality and quantity. In order to be a great trial
attorney, you have to take a lot of cases to court. In order to sign
great cases, you have to get a lot of leads. In order to get those
leads, you have to market yourself—and in order to truly understand what good marketing is, you have to do a lot of it.

The problem is that if you are like most attorneys, *you were not trained in marketing.* That's perfectly understandable: you went to law school, not business school. You also face an even greater challenge as a personal injury attorney specifically, because your niche is the most saturated area of the law. The cost of advertising in your market is exponentially higher because of the extreme levels of competition.

Because marketing is so costly, yours simply *has to* generate leads. You can't afford to waste your advertising dollars—they are too precious. But although you recognize that you have to market your business, you may not know how much to invest, or where, or *how to stand out.*

P. T. Barnum said it best: "No one ever made a difference by being like everyone else."

You may have hired an SEO, pay-per-click, or TV production company to help with your marketing strategy. Most of those companies, however, don't truly consider one of the most important components of marketing, which is:

How are you different?

You can flood every marketing channel there is, but if you don't spend some time thinking about how you are different from the litany of other PI attorneys out there, the chances are slim that people will remember you in the future...and if no one remembers your name, they can't hire you.

If you practiced a different area of law—say, an intellectual property lawyer or business lawyer—and you were the only one in your city, you would always stand out. You would automatically generate business, because if you're the only option, then *you are the best by default.*

When potential clients have more choices, however—such as in the crowded field of personal injury law—you have to do more to be distinctive. Clients are in pain. They need help. You are the best person to help solve their pain, but that only matters if they know who you are and how to find you. After all, the best-kept secret is broke...and not helping anyone.

Throughout the book, you will see boxes like this with quotes from GOAT PI attorneys who have appeared on my *Personal Injury Mastermind* podcast.

Here's our first **GOAT Quote:**

Chad Dudley of Dudley DeBosier, one of the top firms in the nation, joined me on episode 181 of my podcast to say, "In a healthy personal injury firm, the top 5 percent of their cases typically generates around 50 percent of their revenue."

A business exists to generate a profit. If you have no leads, which come from marketing, you have no profit—and therefore no business. Successful firms use marketing not just to get more cases, but to get *better* ones.

(At the end of each GOAT Quote, you'll see
a QR code like the one here, which you can
scan to listen to the full podcast episode.)

WHAT MAKES SOMEONE THE GOAT?

Tom Brady. Serena Williams. Lionel Messi. Michael Phelps. Muhammad Ali.

What do they have in common? All of these people are the GOAT in their sport.

But what does it mean to be the GOAT? Literally, it means the *greatest of all time*. So, what makes someone the greatest? What are some of the commonalities shared among all GOATs?

First, of course, a GOAT has to have talent. You can't just call yourself the greatest; you have to show up and actually *be the best*. That doesn't mean a GOAT is born that way, though. To become the best, a GOAT shows up consistently, day in and day out. Look at the longevity of LeBron James or Tom Brady; they continued playing at an elite level well after their peers had retired.

Second, GOATs continually compete and strive to get better. As lifelong learners, they analyze their performance to see how they can improve—even (or perhaps *especially*) after becoming the GOAT. This approach is as necessary in marketing as it is in sports. It may seem like a 1 percent improvement isn't much by itself, but when those incremental improvements compound over time, that's what really sets you apart.

Finally, GOATs are resilient. When something knocks them down, they bounce back up, usually bigger and better than before. GOATs don't consider setbacks to be failures; they look at those moments as opportunities to learn and to grow.

And that's great news for you. Why? Because it means that even if you are not the GOAT in your market yet, by following the lessons you will learn in this book as well as the examples of other high-achieving personal injury attorneys, you have the opportunity to achieve GOAT status.

Just as in *Highlander*, however, *there can only be one.*

That doesn't mean only one personal injury attorney can *ever* be the GOAT, just that there can only be one *greatest of all time* in each market.

Think about it: we can debate whether Michael Jordan, LeBron James, or Kobe Bryant is the best basketball player of all time. Jordan redefined the sport in the 1980s and '90s; at his peak, he was the best offensive *and* defensive player in the NBA. LeBron is the NBA's all-time leading scorer and an amazing all-around player. Kobe was the all-time leading scorer for the Lakers, and he was the first guard in NBA history to play twenty seasons.

If you ask me, LeBron is the actual GOAT. He has more than 965 wins (that's just as of writing this sentence—he keeps getting more all the time), compared to Jordan's 706. Some people argue, "Jordan would have won more if he would have played longer, blah blah blah." Well, he didn't! We're not living in hypothetical land; we can only look at the actual results. And those results show that LeBron is the best.

There are other greats too: Steph Curry rules at shooting. Magic was a master playmaker. Until LeBron broke his record in 2023, Kareem Abdul-Jabbar held the honor of highest scorer for nearly forty years. Each of these players deserves their spot on the list, whether for destroying records or dominating in a particular position.

So, while you may already be good—or even great—keep reading to learn how you can level up to become *the greatest* in your market.

MARKETING IS EVERYTHING

It's still early in the book, so it's cool if you're sitting there wondering, *Chris, what the hell does marketing actually mean?*

Seth Godin defines marketing as "the generous act of helping someone solve a problem. Their problem."

A more common dictionary definition might be that marketing is simply the process of attracting prospective clients to your firm.

But I would argue that marketing goes beyond that. Most people think marketing is about awareness and leads, but really marketing is *everything*. Everything you do to help people learn and remember your name—every activity your firm undertakes to promote the hiring of your services—is marketing.

If you were to take a Marketing 101 class, you would learn the Five Ps of Marketing: product, price, promotion, place, and people. But these terms are product-oriented, and you're not selling a product; you're providing a service, and that means marketing *yourself*.

Instead of the Five Ps, I like to divide marketing into three components, which I call PEP:

- Prospective clients
- Existing clients
- Past clients

To be the GOAT of marketing, put a little PEP in your step!

Marketing to prospective clients includes all the channels I will discuss later in the book. For existing clients, it may not feel like marketing to provide them with excellent service, but it is—ensuring they have a positive experience makes them more likely to leave you a great review. And you guessed it: that review is part of marketing. Finally, you can market to past clients to activate them into referring your firm to other people they know who may find themselves in similar situations and could benefit from your offerings. See what I mean? It's all marketing!

While there will always be new advancements, and technology is constantly evolving, I want to talk to you about the age-old principles of marketing: how to stand out, how to market with PEP, and how to play the attention game.

WHY LISTEN TO ME?

Why should you listen to me when it comes to marketing your personal injury law firm?

It's simple: I specialize in your specific struggle. I am the owner and CEO of a digital marketing agency that specializes in helping personal injury attorneys grow their practices, and I've been doing it in the most ruthless markets for well over a decade.

I'm also the author of *Niching Up*, a book about choosing a niche—which you have already done by choosing personal injury (and even further, by specializing in subsets such as workers' comp, traumatic brain injuries, medical malpractice, or truck accidents). I choose to work with PI attorneys like you because the personal injury market is so saturated that it demands expertise, which is a form of value—and value is profit.

Additionally, the attorneys I work with *need* my help. The way you market yourself shapes how you are perceived. Just like I'm not here to write the second-best legal marketing book, I want to help you make your firm the *best-marketed* firm.

Not that long ago, it was considered taboo for professionals to market themselves (for example, by advertising on TV or billboards). Some of the old guard still think that advertising isn't beneficial—but I want to flip that narrative. Personal injury attorneys provide an *incredibly valuable* service, and in order for you to help the people who need you, those people first need to be able to find you.

You protect the rights of individuals who are at risk of being manipulated and deceived by insurance companies. You work with people who are experiencing some of the worst days of their lives—and you do it all with empathy and understanding.

In episode 178 of my podcast, I spoke with Patrick Salvi Sr. of Salvi, Schostok & Pritchard—one of the largest firms in Chicago. Patrick has more than three hundred multimillion-dollar victories, and he reminded me why I work with PI attorneys.

Patrick started his career in criminal defense, but most of his clients were criminals, so he felt like he was on the wrong side of the law. That's why he switched to practicing personal injury law. As a PI attorney, his clients aren't criminals, or even alleged criminals; they're people who have been injured and just need help.

As part of our discussion, I asked Patrick what he would tell an injured party who needs to hire an attorney when they ask why they should choose him. Here's what he had to say:

> When I am interviewing a potential client in a situation, usually they're just very up-front and tell me that they're speaking with other firms.

Number one, I spend the time that's necessary to get to know them and show sincere empathy to their situation. I truly and sincerely say to them, "I'm so sorry to meet you under these circumstances." They've lost a loved one, or they've suffered a terrible injury, or a loved one has—a spouse or a child.

And then what I try to do is to, in a sincere fashion, persuade them that they've come to the right place. I tell them, and I mean it when I say I'm not a high-pressure salesperson, "The other firms that you've talked to are excellent, but I have to say we probably have the largest verdicts and settlements in the city and in the state, and we're very experienced with regards to the particular situation that you're in. Although it's going to take a lot of work and know-how, it's not a particularly complex case. You've come to the right place. Now, I'm biased, but I don't think there's anyone that is going to do a better job than myself and my law firm, and we're ready to get to work on the case right now. Right now." I mean what I say; I'm not trying to bamboozle them. I honestly believe that they found the right person. They're in the right place. They don't need to do any more. They've found me.

You've probably had a similar conversation, letting a client know that they've found the right person and the best firm for their case—that they're in the right hands. Well, I want to do the same for you. *You are in the right place.* I am the best person to help *you* become the GOAT in your market.

I know some of you might be wondering, *Is this just Chris's thinly veiled attempt to advertise his business?*

I mean, a little, sure. After all, I do run an agency that specializes in helping people like you. Obviously, I would love an opportunity to work with every hungry, ready-to-grow attorney I can find.

So, if buying and reading this book encourages you to reach out and set an appointment for us to talk, that's great!

But if you don't? That is A-OK too. There are other great digital agencies out there, and there are attorneys who are capable of doing it all by themselves.

Chances are, many of you reading this won't execute on what I'm telling you here. For those of you who will, fantastic! You're going to experience the benefits that come from learning this firsthand.

But if you want someone else to execute for you, Rankings.io is *the* digital marketing agency to meet your needs.

FROM GOOD TO GOAT

This book is intended to be a user's guide for marketing for personal injury attorneys. I'm not going to talk about how to run your firm's finances, its legal aspects, or even the sales side of things.

By now, it should be clear that I'm talking about marketing for the *personal injury* space, specifically. If you're in a different area of law (or a different business altogether), this advice may not apply in the same way. Although many principles of marketing are general, personal injury attorneys in particular have to be GOAT-level marketers. According to business strategists W. Chan Kim and Renée Mauborgne, there are two kinds of markets: "red oceans" packed with competitors fighting for share, and "blue oceans"—niches that you create for yourself, transcending competition. You are currently swimming in a red ocean; this book will teach you some of the principles to create your own blue ocean.

Most business books are generic; they don't offer specialized guidance for a certain industry, and especially not a specific niche. The information here, however, comes from your peers and the biggest players in the game. The examples I use throughout are from real-life personal injury attorneys I've worked with and/or had as guests on my podcast, *Personal Injury Mastermind*. Don't just take it from me! You'll hear from tons of PI attorneys who are actively playing—and winning—the marketing game.

You're going to learn:

- How direct response and branding are like speed dating versus marriage
- How to be like Norm walking into Cheers—everyone is gonna know your name

- How to put your marketing dollars to work
- How to differentiate your firm from your competition
- How to find the clients who will chase you like you allegedly chase ambulances
- How to make sure your billboard message doesn't land like a turd in a punchbowl
- How to use your height to dunk on the competition
- Whether you should buy or DIY
- Which marketing channels are making it rain for PI attorneys today
- How to ensure your marketing efforts are effective—not a guaranteed piece of crap

Here's the secret: technically, all marketing works, but its degree of effectiveness is determined by your strategy and execution. If you use the tools in this book, your marketing will work *better*. You can be good—or even great—at any of the component pieces, but it's only when you add them all together that you benefit from the multiplier effect and can rise to GOAT status.

You may be decent at some aspects of marketing—or you may pay someone who is decent—but you *need* this information to be the greatest of all time in your market. It's not enough to just be a *good* PI attorney, because there are lots of good PI attorneys out there. My goal is to help you continue on your journey to be seen as the best.

PERSONAL INJURY LAWYER MARKETING

At the end of the book, you'll find a series of questions to evaluate where you currently stand. (I'll give you a hint for the test: if you're not answering yes to all of these questions, you're not yet the GOAT!) If you don't have everything in place yet, don't worry—after reading this book, you'll know what to do. Go back through and reread sections as necessary to make sure you don't miss any elements.

Ready to take the first step from good to GOAT? Chapter 1 will reveal whether or not you add up, with the Marketing Equation.

THE MARKETING EQUATION

"Get out of your way, turn off the fear,
and fucking go. What are you waiting for?"

—GINA ZAPANTA OF Z.A. LAWYERS
Personal Injury Mastermind podcast episode 180

T HERE ARE TWO BASIC TYPES OF MARKETING: DIRECT response and branding. Direct response is a marketing tactic with the goal of encouraging an immediate response from consumers in order to quickly generate new leads. Brand marketing, on the other hand, is the process of establishing and growing a relationship between your firm and your prospective clients over time.

We can look at the two in a number of ways:

Direct response is like swiping through a dating app, playing the numbers game just to ensure you'll have a date on Friday night. Branding, on the other hand, is about attracting the right person to eventually become your spouse.

Direct response is like day-trading—evaluating a stock on its individual returns, measured during a short-term window, with all the accompanying volatility. Branding is a long-term investment in a stock that pays dividends and may split.

If marketing were baseball, direct response would be the closer coming in to pitch only an inning or two before burning out, while branding would be a starting pitcher who could carry you for most of the innings (or even the whole ball game).

In real estate terms, direct response would be house flipping to get an immediate return, whereas branding would be buying a property to hold it and earn more through rental income, appreciation, and long-term cash flow.

Direct response is a tummy tuck, while branding is a sustainable diet and exercise regimen.

Essentially, direct response marketing represents a short-term *push*. It's both tactical and transactional, paying for conversions in your funnel, and it's all about interruption. Branding, however, offers a longer-term *pull*. It establishes a message about your firm's benefits and creates a distinct identity in the market for your audience. It's strategic, it's about perception, and it's designed to build relationships.

Google Ads are a form of direct response; TV ads are a form of branding. Most branding is sold based on CPM—the cost per thousand impressions. Direct response is typically measured by cost per lead. Because this is a straightforward calculation, direct response is also much easier to measure.

Branding, on the other hand, is more difficult to gauge accurately—how do you weigh the cost of a potential client reading reviews online before making a decision, comparing you to your competitors? How do you measure their perception of you on social media? Buyers don't have one direct path of conversion; they go through many avenues to make purchasing decisions, because consumers are more educated on how to perform research nowadays. In some cases (as with members of Gen Z, for example), they don't even go to Google—they perform their searches on social media platforms. Because of these changes in buying behavior, it has become more difficult to quantify the effect of marketing, particularly branding.

However, direct response may cost you more than branding to acquire a client, because with direct response, a client doesn't *know* you. Time is our most valuable asset, and with direct response, you are effectively buying time; it has more immediate effects, so it costs more to implement. Branding engages investigative clients weighing their options, which is a longer-term pursuit. This is also why branding can deliver higher-value cases and referrals.

Ultimately, *all* marketing works, given enough time and/or money. You can spend more money to get more immediate results with direct response or spend more time and get more returns over the long term with branding (though it still requires money as well).

But how can you be more efficient and effective with your marketing?

Well, that depends on your firm. Which do you want to have as your larger up-front investment: time or cost? Direct response will have a higher up-front cost, but it will generate results in less time. Branding will cost less per conversion in the long term, but it takes more time to develop perception and an identity in a market.

My goal here is not to push you in one direction or the other, toward direct response or branding. Instead, you have to decide based on what your firm's goals and needs are. If you need immediate transactions and want clients *now*—and you're willing (and able) to pay a higher cost per conversion—then focusing primarily on direct response is likely your best choice. If you're investing for the long term (and can afford to play the long game), then you should put a portion of your budget toward branding to obtain that lower cost per acquisition.

Overall, you need a balance of the two to support the current and future needs of your firm.

BUY YOUR WHISKEY BY THE BARREL, NOT THE BOTTLE

Many firms dilute their efforts to the point of making little to no impact. They'll get a couple of billboards, do a little SEO, and maybe try a radio spot, but on the whole, it doesn't add up to much.

From a cost perspective, you really benefit from economy of scale. For example, if you're doing Google Ads, bidding for just a city radius is more expensive than bidding for the whole state or even the entire US. The more you expand and the more you bid, the cheaper your individual cost per lead. This allows you to buy attention at a discounted rate.

As of 2019, Alexander Shunnarah had 2,500 billboards across the southeastern United States (at this point, he likely has more than 3,000). Depending on where you are, a single billboard may cost you somewhere in the $5,000 range. On the other hand, if you purchase multiple billboards at once, you will likely receive a discount. As that discount will likely scale as your quantity purchased increases, it would be foolish to try to acquire 2,500 billboards by making 2,500 separate, individual purchases. You'd be better off buying them by, say, the tens or hundreds at a time, if you could.

The same is true with radio, TV, and SEO. If you only do a few blog posts per month, you won't have enough content to cut through the noise. You need more like a hundred blogs per month to truly make an impact in rank.

When you are first starting out, you are likely undercapital-ized and without much of a marketing budget, so you have to do things that don't typically scale—networking, shaking hands, meeting people on a one-to-one basis. Instead of spending money, you spend *time* getting in front of people so they begin to know your name. This is where network marketing can be very effective.

Once you start to introduce capital, the quickest way to get visibility is to pay for existing distribution—such as through TV ads and paid social.

Ultimately, the long-term way to lower your costs is to create your own assets. By doing so, you also create a moat around distribution that your competitors don't have access to, whether that's creating your own podcast, having a website that ranks really well and does content marketing effectively, building a giant email list, or even owning an office building that is centrally located in a prominent, visible area with good foot traffic.

THE EXPONENTIAL POWER OF MARKETING

Marketing is a linear equation: the higher your input, the more output you receive. The more marketing you do, the more visibility you receive.

When selecting a channel, you can't just dabble; you need to go all in and focus on your chosen marketing method to be effective. Oftentimes this is why SEO "doesn't work" for clients. If you commit a few months of time and thousands of dollars in resources, but you expect immediate results, you may find yourself turning off the SEO spigot right before it begins to flow. SEO has breakthrough moments, and if you tap out before you can break through (you've acquired enough backlinks, you've received good reviews, you've written enough quality content, etc.), but your competitors keep going? Well, now you're even further behind than you were in the first place. You need to pick a lane and commit to it. A large part of success in marketing comes from consistency and repetition.

However, there is also a nonlinear component to marketing, which comes in the exponential form of referrals. You are introduced to one person, who introduces you to two others, each of whom introduces you to five more people. Because this process is nonlinear, it is more difficult to measure, and the cost per lead may ultimately be lower than if you evaluate your marketing efforts solely from a direct-response standpoint.

Strategies for obtaining client referrals include asking for referrals, gathering reviews, and increasing visibility in your market. Peer referrals come from speaking at conferences, hosting a podcast, and other methods to gain recognition among your peers for your craft and particular expertise. Bob Simon of the Simon Law Group, for example, is a trial attorney known for spine injury cases. Dawn Smith of Smith Clinesmith is an expert in nursing-home abuse cases. David Craig of Craig, Kelley & Faultless is *the* expert on trucking injuries. These attorneys chose these specific niches to be known for their craft and expertise. If you are an expert in your craft, other attorneys will refer clients to you. There are typically two reasons for peer referrals: if the case is outside their territory, jurisdiction, or area of law, or if they can refer to someone and that individual can generate more revenue and a higher case value as co-counsel than they could on their own.

GOAT QUOTE

In episode 4 of *Personal Injury Mastermind*, "Using Emotional Intelligence to Boost Your Firm and Client Experience," Larry Nussbaum of Nussbaum Law Group says:

> I'm also a big believer that your best referral source is always going to be your current clients and your prior clients. I've had many cases where somebody comes to me third and nobody would take the case. I'm looking, and I'm like, why didn't they take it to them? I'm thinking, all right, they're thinking that we settled this case for $3,000, the fee's a thousand, they must be so rich or so particular that it's just not worth it to them, but there's no issue with the file. So I worked my ass off on the file. Probably even lose money on the file. But now that person's referred me their mother or their brother. Somebody had a bad injury in the family, so there was a big hit.
>
> I try to help as many people, I try to grow my network as large as I can. I do more than I should probably

for free, but again, I truthfully believe
in karma and then it will all come back.

Go into this work with an abundance mentality. You don't
need to make enemies or feel like referring cases takes something away from you. In fact, your competitors can be some of
your biggest referral partners—to a point.

Let me use my own agency as an example: From zero to $4
million in revenue, we generated a lot of agency referrals. The
moment we passed $4 million in revenue, however, our referrals
evaporated. Suddenly, other firms saw us as a threat. A direct
competitor who had previously sent a number of referrals our
way even told me that we had gotten too big, and that, basically,
it wasn't in their best interest to help us grow any larger.

Once you reach a certain size, people will stop referring to
you because they're afraid you're taking their same client base.
And hey, that's a good problem to have, right?

However, for that reason—and because referrals can come
and go—the flow of leads can feel like feast or famine. But it
doesn't have to be that way: for maximum results, you want to
include a blend of both linear and nonlinear elements. By effectively marketing your firm, you can generate your own cases
and bring in the referrals that help you become the GOAT in
your market.

IT'S A CLICHÉ FOR A REASON:
YOU GOTTA SPEND MONEY TO MAKE MONEY

People frequently ask me, "How much should I invest in my marketing?"

In the book *Ready, Fire, Aim: Zero to $100 Million in No Time Flat,* author Michael Masterson teaches that businesses that have a disproportionate investment in marketing and sales typically grow more than those that don't.

Most businesses need to invest a *minimum* of 20 percent of their top line into their marketing efforts. Darryl Isaacs of Isaacs & Isaacs, for example, uses the recommendation of anywhere from 20 percent to 30 percent—and some years, he invests 40 percent. In an interview I had with him on episode 134 of *Personal Injury Mastermind*, he explained:

> I don't think you can invest enough, because think of it: everything you can invest in, you've got an inventory of cases, they're all future dollars...Let's say my cost per case for pay-per-click is $3,000 a case, but my cost per case on TV ads is $2,300, and my cost per case through LSA [local service ads] is $700. Gosh, I'd love to have the $700 all day long, but I'm still going to take the $3,000 case, because my average fee is $15,000, so I'm still making money...I think a lot of people get pigeonholed and say, "I'm only going to spend this." I think you just have to take your overall budget and

make sure when you add everything up, what's your overall cost per case. As long as it's pretty dispro-
portionate under what your revenue is, you're
gonna make [money].

If you are generating your own cases, as opposed to receiving
peer referrals, you need to spend at least 20 percent of your budget on marketing, because the personal injury field is so saturated. It's too competitive to go any lower. Without spending at
least that much, you can't garner enough attention and awareness; you simply won't be known, because your signal won't be
able to cut through all the noise.

But again, consider your firm's goals. Do you want to have
a lifestyle firm, to feed the family? Or do you want to grow,
make an impact, and be wealthy? The decision is yours, but you
shouldn't expect to spend less than 20 percent and still experience the necessary growth to become a large firm.

Additionally, the percentage of your revenue devoted to marketing needs to grow as your firm grows; it's not a strict budget
item that stays consistent. The largest firms invest 40 percent
to 50 percent (or even more) toward marketing, because that's
what is necessary to continue to stand out in an overcrowded
field. Initially, you may look at investing more heavily in direct
response to get more immediate returns, but some portion of
your investment should *always* go toward the brand. Over time,
as you increase your investment, you will also increase the

— PERSONAL INJURY LAWYER MARKETING —

proportion of marketing going toward branding to support your longer-term goals.

As Henry Ford said, "A man who stops advertising to save money is like a man who stops a clock to save time."

PUTTING IT ALL TOGETHER

As I explained at the beginning of the chapter, you need a mix of direct response and branding to get the best results from your marketing efforts. You also need to spend money to make money—but the money you spend to capture the attention of one client can become exponential if it also generates referrals.

Luis Scott joined me on episode 106 of *Personal Injury Mastermind*, "Rethinking Referrals to Help You Scale." Here's how he thinks about the amount spent to acquire a client versus the amount earned when that client refers others:

> If you were to look at our cost of acquisition for TV or cost of acquisition for radio or cost of acquisition for billboards, you would say it's a monumental failure. You would actually conclude that, because how can you be paying $10,000 to acquire a case? Well, the reason is because if you take the approach that that person is going to turn into three clients, then you know you're not paying $10,000 for a case—you're paying $10,000 for three cases.

— 28 —

If I spent $1 million in marketing and I only made $1 million in revenue, to me that's a win because the upsell is the referral. If I spent $1 million in marketing and I only make $1 million from that, directly attributed to that marketing, but I generate three referrals from each client I got from marketing—that's the win...If you can generate referrals from what marketing delivers, which is what I call "width building," then you are going to drive depth in your organization. If marketing delivers let's say a thousand cases a year but you can turn that into three thousand cases because two thousand are by referral, that is how you win—that is how you lower your cost of acquisition.

I don't consider our firm a big settlement firm, yet last year we had nine seven-figure cases...But those cases came through referrals of people who came through radio station advertisements, TV advertisements...I want to make sure that our marketing is leading to more people, because more people lead to more referrals, and more referrals mean you get more seven-figure cases in the long run, and it just continues to build the brand.

Now that you know you need to invest, and you have an idea of how much you should be spending, what's your strategy?

The rest of the book will look at how to get the most from your marketing—beginning with chapter 2, which focuses on the best way to position your firm to stand out in your market.

2

POSITIONING
MORE INTERESTING THAN MISSIONARY

"[If] you start projecting out there and putting out there that this is what we love working on, this is what we do, this is what we're experts in...that's how people find you."

–CHRISTINA HAGEN OF HAGEN NARES
Personal Injury Mastermind podcast episode 189

I MAGINE FOR A MOMENT THAT YOUR PERSONAL INJURY law firm is a lemonade stand. You sell all-organic, freshly squeezed, small-batch, icy cold lemonade on the warmest summer days, just when people walking by are hot, sweaty, and thirsty. Sounds perfect, right?

Well, here's the rub: your lemonade stand is located on a busy street *lined* with lemonade stands. People can't walk two feet without encountering yet another glass of lemonade. So how is your lemonade going to stand out?

All the stands sell lemonade, but as people walk down the street, they can see the differences between them: some sell frozen lemonade, others offer more than one size, some offer cherry and strawberry lemonade, and still others may sell their lemonade for a little less. Some decorate their lemonade stands with funny pictures and clever sayings; others go more upscale and offer a top-shelf lemon-squeezing experience. Maybe another lemonade stand offers delivery, so people don't even have to make the effort and sacrifice of showing up at the lemonade stand; their frosty, sweet-tart beverage is brought straight to their hot little hands. Others may offer different payment options, accepting credit cards, Venmo, or Apple Pay.

In today's landscape, where everyone has a mobile device in their hand or pocket, and with the ensuing changes to buyer behavior, all businesses are on the same street—they're all online. That applies to personal injury attorneys too. Your law firm is located on the same block as every other law firm in America: on Google Street.

Given the crowded playing field, ask yourself: *How is my personal injury law firm different from all the others?*

IN A WORLD OF PIGEONS, BE A PEACOCK

When deciding to hire a personal injury attorney, clients have many options. You need to find a way to be different, to stand out from the pack, because you don't just want to be *a* choice—you want to be *the* choice. There are only so many cases, so many leads to capture and convert. The best way to convert those consumers is to make your name known; this is referred to as *positioning*.

If you don't stand out, you may not convert as much business. You may have fewer opportunities to hit those exceptional cases that have a lot of value. Hell, without positioning yourself to stand out in the market, you likely won't have the cash flow to support your business. Remember the saying that the best-kept secret is broke? You could be the best personal injury attorney in the world, but if no one knows about you, you're not going to have any clients to keep you in business.

Positioning is the beginning of the funnel, of the flywheel, of being known. Previously, a consumer would just Google "best personal injury attorney in [city]" and then make a decision. Now, they're going to read reviews, go to social media, and have private conversations. It's critical that you have professional positioning and continuity across all platforms.

Positioning for personal injury law firms can be particularly challenging. Not only are you competing in a crowded market, you also want to avoid positioning yourself based on offering the lowest price—price cutting is just a race to the bottom, and as Seth Godin says, "The problem with the race to the bottom is that you just might win." If you sacrifice your margin, you also sacrifice your ability to be profitable and attract top talent. Additionally, the standard consumer typically doesn't focus on pricing in their decision because they've seen so many firms positioned with "free consultations" and "you only pay if we win."

> I work with more than three hundred personal injury firms, and I performed considerable research for this book—and I just haven't seen fee discounts done effectively. But I'm happy to be wrong! If you position yourself based on pricing and have found success with this technique, email me at chris@rankings.io.

In fact, if the normal fee is 33 to 40 percent, I would generally suggest going *higher* than 33 percent. This choice shows that you know you're worth it, you're an expert, and you can get maximum value—and it also allows you to hire top talent and do a better job because you have more resources.

So, if you aren't positioning yourself based on price, how *should* you position your firm?

The answer likely depends on the type of firm you have (or want to have). Are you a litigating firm that wants to try cases for maximum value? If so, then don't position yourself to throw out a net and haul in all the cases you can get; instead, look at value over volume, with more stringent case criteria. In your positioning, you will want to highlight your case results—the seven-, eight-, or even nine-figure amounts won for your clients.

If you're a volume-based shop, on the other hand, you'll have many practice areas and many ways to cast the net and capture cases. You're not litigating them, so you can settle many of them or refer them out to a litigating firm. A non-litigating firm may not typically have cases with large winnings—but they can instead stand out by highlighting the number of clients they've helped. Volume is social proof; consumers typically choose the dentist who has done a thousand procedures over one who has only done a few.

Your positioning also depends on where you want cases to come from and who you're marketing to. For example, some litigating firms will want to highlight both the monetary amounts they've won for clients and their star trial attorney as the expert, because they want peer referrals. By contrast, settlement firms tend not to receive as many referrals, because the value is lower, so they would highlight their expertise more directly to the consumer (rather than to other attorneys or firms).

Settlement firms work by using a similar strategy every time: they go in and get their clients a settlement, which is usually lower than potential winnings at trial—but also notably faster. In general, settlement firms treat individuals like customers, widgets, or cogs in the assembly line. They're trying to solve for the average.

Litigating, on the other hand, is more bespoke, and every case presents a blank canvas. Litigating attorneys typically have their clients' best interest at heart (which is not to say that all settlement firms do not). They tend to have a lower volume of cases because each one requires large amounts of time, attention, and detail to get the maximum value...but the payoff is worth it. Their clients choose them to get fair compensation, so if trial attorneys don't get the right offer, they'll take the case to court. They treat individuals as humans with feelings and emotions, not just cogs in a machine.

You can think of settlement firms as the Ford assembly line and litigating firms as creating a custom-designed Rolls-Royce. In my opinion, as consolidation occurs and data and artificial intelligence become more prominent, demand for litigation and expertise will increase and, therefore, so will competition around the commoditized settlement mill.

But don't just take my word for it. Michael Alder of AlderLaw shares some thoughts in episode 185 of *Personal Injury Mastermind*:

> Well, first of all, what's [the firm owner's] mindset? What's their goal? Are they interested in...making as much money as possible, or are they interested in helping their clients get as much money as possible? There are many firms that the primary interest is how do the owners or the people at the

top make the most money? And they treat clients differently. They treat them as widgets, right? They don't need to talk to the client, because they're a widget and it's just a bag of money that I need to extract out of that case.

If you instead have a mindset of "I will make plenty of money if I maximize the value for my client," now just that mindset change increases the quality of your legal representation.

I know some trial attorneys don't like the so-called "settlement firms." But they do like the referrals they get from them. It's challenging to fish for just high-value commercial policy cases. To use Alex Shunnarah's analogy, "Not every minnow can be a marlin." In most cases, you need to fish where all the fish live to have a chance to catch a marlin; there's an ecosystem to this work.

Additionally, trial attorneys tend to have a sense of pride in not advertising. They will confidently say, "I don't spend anything on marketing! I don't have to pay to advertise, because I get all my business through referrals."

But of course they do! They're all paying for advertising and marketing—they're just not paying for their own advertising. Instead, they're paying for someone else's (the referrer's) when they pay for a referral. That person or firm pays plenty to advertise and then, when they

> *have a case they can't try, they refer it to the trial attor-*
> *ney who doesn't pay to market his firm—but who* does
> *pay 33 percent to 50 percent as a finder's fee.*

HOW TO STAND OUT

In his book *Fireproof*, Mike Morse says, "Cherry Garcia beats vanilla." So, what flavor are you serving up?

Because consumers have many options for personal injury firms, you need to differentiate yourself. Some of the possible methods include:

- Niching up into a subspecialty of personal injury law
- Appealing to a certain demographic
- Being entertainingly memorable
- Highlighting your experience
- Showcasing how often you win and/or how much value your clients have received
- Offering greater convenience to your clients
- Utilizing cutting-edge technology
- Providing a world-class customer experience

Let's take a closer look at how to approach each of these, as well as some examples of law firms that stand out in each area.

Niching Up (I Literally Wrote a Book on It!)

One way to change your positioning is by finding a more specific niche in a practice area of the law.

This method for standing out is typically better suited for litigating firms because of their focus and expertise. They drill down to understand the material and have the competency to get maximum value (whereas non-litigating firms stay higher-level because they tend to settle cases or refer them out).

GOAT QUOTE

On episode 250 of my podcast, Steven Gursten of Michigan Auto Law asks an important question about when to niche:

> [I]s now the time to start exploring other areas of practice, other areas of law that are much less competitive, much more lucrative, much more "blue ocean," so to speak? The best time to plant a tree is yesterday, but the second-best time to plant a tree is today. And I'd much rather be entering new areas of practice now than try and do it, let's say, five years from now when everybody's already losing their heads and desperate and everyone's trying to do it all at once.

Joe Fried of Fried Goldberg is an example of someone who stands out by niching up. Personal injury is already a niche of the legal industry, but then within personal injury, he further focuses on truck accidents. No one knows more about a trucking manual than Joe. He's well known, so if someone needs to refer a trucking case, they're likely going to send it to him.

GOAT QUOTE

On episode 63 of the *Personal Injury Mastermind* podcast, Joe Fried says, "I don't think success is born from balance. Success is born from concentration."

Another example is Ben Crump, who is known as *the* civil rights attorney. If someone has a civil rights issue, they want to go to him.

Law Tigers focuses on motorcycle accidents. Some people specialize in deck collapses, burns, or medical malpractice.

Dawn Smith of Smith Clinesmith came on episode 235 of the podcast to talk about how she found her niche as an advocate for nursing-home abuse victims, explaining, "My partner and I started doing some asbestos litigation, but he was always doing nursing-home abuse. Based on the national reach that we had with the asbestos practice and some of the contacts that we've made over the years, we really felt like we could make the biggest impact doing these types of cases only, across the country, because it's really an underserved population."

All of these are examples of niches within personal injury. When you niche up, you're not just a personal injury attorney—you become a specialist within the field of personal injury law. You can take any of these specialties, create a niche, and do much better than you otherwise would, because you'll get referrals and know how to maximize your marketing spend. When you choose a niche, you have a more specific target, so you can speak directly to the people in that niche. That specificity shapes your marketing plan. For instance, if you're going to be *the* bicycle attorney, then it would be smart to sponsor and attend bicycle events or partner up with bicycle manufacturers and give away branded helmets.

GOAT QUOTE

I spoke with Corey Quinn, former CMO of Scorpion Marketing, who shared the keys to effectively niching up:

> There [are] three elements that go into success, and I
> call it the deep specialization strategy.

Number one is having focus, and focus is saying yes to one thing [while] at the same time saying no to a lot of other things—so being really intentional about what you want to focus in on when it comes to who you're serving.

Number two is having a strategy, which is a massive action plan built to achieve a big goal. So you have to know what you're trying to go after and put a lot of energy into focusing your effort and resources into achieving a specific goal.

And then the third one is care, which is all about finding an audience that you want to serve, that you actually care about. Because we live in a very competitive market today where people are searching for niches left and right. They're throwing money here, throwing money there. And what becomes a signal in the market is when an attorney really shows that they care about this audience. They may have a personal connection, they may have a familial connection to this audience, they may have other types of connections, but there's a level of care that allows them to break through the noise, the marketing noise, and communicate to that audience much more authentically in a way that stands out much better than not caring.

Who Do You Serve?

You can also position yourself based on your own demographics or the demographics you serve to help your firm stand out. We'll dig deeper into this strategy in the next chapter, on targeting. People do business with those they know, like, and trust—and they most trust people who are similar to them. For example, you may want to highlight if you are a woman-owned or minority-owned firm. Definitely mention if you speak another language, because clients who speak that language will be more comfortable with an attorney who can talk to them in their native tongue. Los Defensores, for example, is a firm that primarily serves clients from Mexico and spends over $20 million a year to advertise on Spanish-language television networks.

GOAT QUOTE

On episode 116 of the *Personal Injury Mastermind* podcast, "Breaking into the Bilingual Market," Liel Levy of Nanato Media shares his thoughts on the importance of standing out for your demographic:

> It's all about really tailoring the client experience, where your Spanish-speaking clients can come to the law firm and get taken care of without language

being a roadblock. So how do you take care of that? By having bilingual staff, Spanish speakers that actually speak Spanish fluently handling the intake, being present when they are around at the office, when they come and sign documents, [and,] needless to say, read contracts–those need to be in Spanish and such.

And it goes beyond just the language side of things. You also need to understand how these demographic groups communicate and prefer to interact with your law firm. Many still, even past COVID, prefer to meet in person at offices; that's just the way they are. So the whole idea of virtual consultations and such may not necessarily resonate very well with some segments within the Hispanic market. The other thing to keep in mind is that the Spanish-speaking market is 100 percent mobile–everything that they do is through their mobile device. And many of them, they are not using our emails at all for almost anything. And so when you're trying to send them a Docusign to get them to sign the contract, that may not necessarily be the best way of getting them to do it. You may be better off by sending it through text message or being able to communicate with them via WhatsApp, which they use a lot. So being aware of all of those nuances and adjusting and adapting

your client experience to make it easy
for them to interact with your law firm
are going to be critical and essential.

I once saw a bunch of potheads who were criminal defense attorneys—and they really owned being stoners themselves, which appealed to the people they wanted to reach. John Berry of Berry Law highlights his military service to reach veterans. Michael Gibson—of Michael T. Gibson, P.A., Auto Justice Attorney—includes his wife and kids on his billboards to show how family-oriented he is. Gordon McKernan in Louisiana reaches a religious demographic by praying with clients during consults and giving Bibles to them.

Geography is also a subset of demographics, if regional pride or identity is something that you can emphasize in your marketing (like being from the state of Texas or born in the Bronx). Frank Azar only practices in Colorado, and he positions himself as Colorado's largest personal injury law firm. Jennifer Gore-Cuthbert highlights running a woman-owned firm, and she also positions her firm based on geography, down to the name: Atlanta Personal Injury Law Group. With his thousands of billboards, Alexander Shunnarah is the best-known face in Alabama, which he highlights with his slogan, "Call me, Alabama."

> On The Game Changing Attorney *podcast, Shunnarah*
> *says, "I can't imagine someone else being the most*
> *recognizable person or the number one law firm in*
> *Alabama—not on my watch. I joke around that if I ever*
> *drive in Alabama and somebody has a larger law firm or*
> *is more popular than I am, or is more branded, I'm just*
> *going to jump off a bridge!"*

You may even position yourself using your demographic along with another aspect: "Car Crash Ash" of Rawlins Law, for example, highlights the female demographic as well as the number of awards she has won (which falls under winning, as described a little later in the chapter, in the section "Money Talks"). The "Car Wreck Cowboy" of Montgomery Law appeals to the "country" demographic, as well as offering entertainment.

Are You Not Entertained?

Another way of making yourself memorable is by using an entertaining firm name, slogan, or advertisement.

Take TopDog Law, for example—that's certainly not the name of your typical law firm. In fact, James Helm came on episode 227 of the podcast to talk about the importance of being memorable:

I want to tell everybody first and foremost just how nervous I was calling our law firm TopDog Law. I still remember I went to my first-ever legal conference, and I'm checking in at the check-in table, and I'm a little intimidated, just even walking in. I don't know what to expect. I'm twenty-eight years old in a room full of like fifty-, sixty-year-old, very wealthy, established lawyers. Felt like I didn't deserve to be in the room. And I get up to the table, and there's this nice older lady who's checking people in. And right as I'm checking in, I'm like, "James from TopDog Law." And I still remember these two lawyers next to me and the look on their face when I said TopDog Law. They were like, it was this scoff.

And at the time, I was ashamed. But over time, and as we've grown the TopDog brand, I look back and think about how contrarian it was to go with a branded name like that. And given that it's so easy to say, easy to spell, easy to remember, I think a large part of our success is due to the name...

I think lawyers have traditionally been very bad at branding their businesses. I mean, every other industry has names that are easy to say, easy to spell, easy to remember. Whereas law firms, the brand wasn't the focus. The brand was basically a bunch of last names that are often hard to spell, hard to remember. And the question becomes, "Who's your lawyer?" "I don't know. I could try to find their business card." Whereas, if your lawyer's TopDog, it's like, "Oh, TopDog. Go to topdoglaw.com." And how many more client referrals are you going to get? And we all know client referrals are the best kind of referrals. Why? Because they're free.

King Aminpour plays up the name King by wearing a gold crown and including a chess king in his logo.

Jim Adler calls himself The Texas Hammer and positions himself as a superhero figure in commercials, charging a semitruck with a sledgehammer. (There's also The Illinois Hammer and The Kentucky Hammer, no relation—but another example of geographic positioning with an entertaining name.)

GOAT QUOTE

Darryl "The Hammer" Isaacs (The Kentucky Hammer) says, "If you want to be known, you gotta do something that makes you stand out."

Jungle Law shows lawyers dressed in Tarzan and Jane costumes, with a cheetah, koala, elephant, or lion. (They are criminal defense attorneys, but that doesn't prevent them from using humor to make their firm memorable.)

Kathleen Martinez of Martinez Immigration dresses in bright pink and has all women in her photos. Her team looks like they're straight out of *Legally Blonde*—and that pop culture reference works, because it's different from all the other dark-suited lawyers. (She also hits the demographic that values working with a woman-owned firm.)

Nobody Wants a Noob

You may choose to stand out by highlighting your experience, such as how long your firm has been in business or the thousands of people you've helped.

Fried Goldberg LLC highlights having over one hundred years of combined experience handling truck accident cases. The team at West Coast Trial Lawyers emphasizes that they're Harvard-educated.

Morgan & Morgan's tagline is "Size matters." They have the humor aspect, but they're also positioning themselves as America's largest personal injury law firm. (Dolman Law Group takes the opposite approach, saying, "Size doesn't matter, unless it comes to your settlement.")

If you can position yourself as an expert, sometimes you don't have to do anything to receive an opportunity. If people are deep-sea diving and they find a treasure, they're going to call in an expert to help them retrieve it. It's the same for trial attorneys: if someone finds the ultimate case, but they know they don't have the experience to do it, they have to find the attorney who does—which means that you want to be that expert.

Money Talks

Value and winning offer another way of differentiating your firm. Highlight the big settlements your clients have received, the number of cases you've won—even winning awards, such as being voted best firm in your area.

Steve Dimopoulos of Dimopoulos Injury Law highlights being voted both the best injury lawyer and the best trial lawyer in Las Vegas. Being voted the best or number one attorney highlights winning and social proof (just remember that, legally, you can't say you're the best—but you can certainly highlight *other people* saying that you are).

Mike Morse positions himself as Michigan's largest personal injury law firm. He's chosen to own Michigan, which is geographic (within demographics), but he's also positioning how much he wins for his clients—his phone number is even 855-MIKE-WINS.

Similarly, Brett Sachs's firm, MVP Accident Attorneys, positions this quality right in their name—MVP shows you're a winner.

GOAT QUOTE

In episode 126 of *Personal Injury Mastermind*, Brett Sachs of MVP Accident Attorneys explains his firm's name:

MVPs excel at their position under extreme circum-stances. They always make it through, no matter what. And they're always a team player...What we love about the MVP brand and what it's done to our firm is it solidified something to believe in. We're not just a law firm or a business. We are something bigger than ourselves.

One of the other reasons why I like the brand of MVP over Sachs Law is that I don't have to be associated with it. The MVP, to me, is the firm, not me, not a face on a billboard. God forbid something happens to me—what do you do with that? I want our clients to always have something to trust and believe in, whether I'm personally here or not. It's super important to me that the attorneys, the case managers, the intake specialists, the receptionist, our controller, our management team, every person that walks into this office is a direct result of our product. And they all deserve to feel like they are the MVP.

Make It Easy

You might stand out based upon the convenience you offer your clients. Some firms don't have any brick-and-mortar locations; they are 100 percent remote. Others may offer multiple locations to choose from, Zoom or phone consultations, meeting the client in person, or 24/7 consultations.

On the Bleeding Edge

Technology is yet another way to stand out. Your firm may analyze the data to know what insurance companies will pitch or to show the likelihood of winning at trial. Some individuals highlight using certain trial software. Leveraging AI may even differentiate you from the competition. If so, make sure everyone knows about it! Anthony Johnson, for example, positions himself as the "techiest" lawyer. On *The Game Changing Attorney* podcast, he says:

> Our challenge as an industry—and as a world—is to figure out how we can understand data on the same level, like leveling the playing field. The legal industry right now is very fragmented. All the technology is different, and every lawyer has a different CRM [customer relation management system] and a different way of doing it, so we've really broken down what these pieces of data are at their core. Like not "What's the jurisdiction?" or "Who's a co-counsel?" but is this a role relationship with the case, you know, from a database perspective? And is that role a person, or is it a group of people, or is it an entity? Because it's all the same thing in the end. So how can you structure this framework that ties in every other platform in the industry? If we can

standardize this framework, we can essentially be the Tower of Babel of the industry—and if we can connect our industry and create some kind of solidarity that actually matched what the defense and the insurance companies have with Colossus and those mechanisms, then we would actually have a level playing field.

GOAT QUOTE

Sean Claggett of Claggett & Sykes says, "Attorneys that are not using data in their cases are taking unnecessary risks."

The Client Is King

Providing great customer service is definitely a way to stand out in a crowded marketplace. Some firms go and meet the prospect at their house. Mickey Fine meets with every single prospect and client, in person, to shake their hand. If Dan Newlin gets a bad review, he tries to resolve the problem face to face.

These are examples of experiences that go above and beyond—and help your name become known among your audience.

GOAT QUOTE

On episode 34 of my podcast, Seth Godin speaks about positioning your firm based around what your clients need:

> If you find a key lying on the ground and you didn't know what lock it fit, it would be worthless...On the other hand, if you have a door you need to open and a locksmith says, "For two hundred bucks, I'll open the door," and you need to get in, you'll happily pay that because that's what you're buying: not a key, but an open door. And so when someone comes to you with a problem, the fact that you're parading around with a bunch of solutions is irrelevant—unless it's the solution they were looking for.

The biggest cases come from referrals because those consumers spend more time researching who is the best. If you take the time to position yourself and become known as the best—whether that's best in your niche, in your area, in a certain demographic, or at providing a specific service—then you'll get those referrals.

IF YOU'VE GOT IT, FLAUNT IT

Once you've determined how to stand out, you want to make sure everyone knows about it—and you tell them by utilizing a unique selling proposition.

A unique selling proposition, or USP, is your differentiator, which you can then use in all of your marketing to highlight what makes your firm different from everyone else's. Without a unique selling proposition, you have to spend more for advertising. In fact, when looking for examples to use in the previous section, I scrolled through so many websites—and the vast majority of them looked the same! Don't be generic; make your firm *unique*.

Settlement firms often don't have a unique selling proposition, so they have to advertise more. They may spend way more money to get in front of people and to get their attention, because everyone's trying to do the same. These firms often struggle to stand out; they're competing in a red ocean. Firms with a unique selling proposition, on the other hand, frequently don't have to advertise as much because they become known through word of mouth.

But that level of success doesn't happen right away. Becoming known, and developing a USP, comes from experience and results. You will typically want to have some experience before you decide upon a unique selling proposition. That's not to say you can't start with one if you identify a hole right out of the gate, but firms often discover these later, rather than creating them at the outset. Morgan & Morgan, for example, couldn't claim the USP of America's largest personal injury law firm from the start; that title came decades later.

At the beginning, you have to be broad. You can't be narrow in your advertising because it needs maximum usage. This is similar to the *Ready, Fire, Aim* approach popularized by Michael Masterson. You launch a personal injury law firm, and then you go broad and try to get everything you can. The focus is on how you can convert and win more.

Once you have that experience and those results under your belt, however, then you're ready to identify what makes your firm unique.

In order to uncover your potential USP, you can ask your team what they find different about working for your firm. You can also survey your clients. Ask them about their experience and why they chose you—and really listen to what they say. If you hear, "It's hard for me to get around, and you were the only one who would come to my house," then your USP may be accessibility. Maybe they say, "I was searching late at night, but you were still available to talk." In that instance, you would highlight your 24/7 consultations. Or someone might explain, "I chose you because I could see that you were the biggest firm, and that sounded like you would be the most powerful—that's who I want fighting for me." You can use those words right on your website!

You can also analyze your customer reviews. Testimonials and success stories are valuable because they show what your customers love about you. See what people are saying more than once, and that's likely something that differentiates you.

Another way of extracting a USP is by auditing your competitors to see what they *don't* highlight. Anything missing from the market is a hole that your firm could potentially fill.

Avoid doing the same thing everyone else is doing. If all the competitors in your market have blue backgrounds on their website, try green or purple. Do something different so it stands out in the minds of the consumers looking at those sites; even your color palette can be a differentiator.

But whatever you do, be authentic. There's only one you, and you need to share that person with the world. If you're boring, be boring! Own that boringness. If you like boxing, wear boxing gloves and advertise with boxers! If you like to shock people, be authentically over-the-top. Take, for example, Thomas J. Henry—his daughter's quinceañera may have cost $6 million and featured performances by Pitbull and Nick Jonas...but he and his family also spent a day driving children with cancer around in their Ferraris to have "over-the-top celebrity day experiences" with the charity Ferrari Kid. Similarly, he may have advertised his firm at the Super Bowl in a commercial showcasing his Learjet, but he also gives away thousands of frozen turkeys for Thanksgiving, even flying in by helicopter to hand them out.

PERSONAL INJURY LAWYER MARKETING

A USP is similar to Todd Brown's concept of a unique mechanism, which he defines as "the unique manner, method, or material that allows the product or service to deliver the desired benefits." A USP is a unique benefit; a unique mechanism is a distinctive way that you achieve your desired outcome. It's how you deliver on the promise. For example, there are generic exercise programs, and then there's P90X and CrossFit. There are plain old diets, and then there's keto and South Beach. What's different about you? What system helps you get results? How does your service deliver the desired outcome?

At one point, Merry Fountain had a unique mechanism where she met every one of her clients at their house. From a value perspective, she decreased the effort required of the consumer to meet with her, and that's a huge factor for some folks.

Or maybe you utilize different trial techniques. Rex Parris, for example, specializes in using Neuro-Linguistic Programming (NLP) and cognitive science in his trials, which you can hear more about in Personal Injury Mastermind *podcast episode 199.*

Tell 'Em with a Tagline

One component of a USP is a tagline. If the goal of a USP is to highlight what makes you distinctive, then a tagline broadcasts what makes you unique to your audience.

But what is a tagline?

A tagline is a short, memorable phrase that represents your firm's brand, values, and personality. The most famous tagline in the legal space is Morris Bart's "One call, that's all." It's short, simple, and represents the ease of working with him. People get overwhelmed at the thought of hiring an attorney; Bart's tagline shows them how little effort the experience can require. They don't have to call around. They won't need to endure being on the phone with a bunch of different people. It implies that with only one call—if it's the right call, to Morris Bart—they will connect with exactly the right person to help them. That's a pretty hefty message packed into just four little words.

GOAT QUOTE

On episode 105 of the *Grow Your Law Firm* podcast, Morris Bart discusses how he first came up with that now-famous tagline:

> Many years ago, there was something new that came
> on television known as infomercials...Some people

call them long-format commercials, but basically it was a thirty-minute pretend show where you tried to sell your product. I was fascinated by infomercials. I was just fascinated by the whole concept, and I would watch those—I've always been a student of marketing, and I've always loved marketing.

So they had an infomercial on at that time...It was called the Grapefruit 45 Diet...The premise was that these brilliant scientists had taken a secret ingredient out of grapefruits, known as pectin, and they had put that in a pill. And by taking this pill at night, while you slept it would dissolve the fat in your body, and in the morning you would simply urinate the fat out. And so then they had all these people come on television who would say, "It was so easy. All I did was I took this simple pill at night and I've lost thirty pounds in the last month, and I'm still eating bacon and steaks and French fries and fried chicken and everything I love, and I'm losing weight."

And I was fascinated by that. So I went and saw my agent and friend in New Orleans...And I went over to Rick's house and I told him, I said, "Rick, you know, I figured out what America wants. They want things quick, simple, easy. They don't want to hear to lose weight, I've got to diet, I've got to exercise, I've got to work hard. No, they just want to take one pill and that's it, then they lose their weight. So we need to adapt that to law. We need to come up with a slogan that's as easy as the Grapefruit 45 Diet."

So we start talking about, well, you know, how does law work? How do people contact a lawyer? Well, they call a lawyer. Okay, so what could be easier? Maybe one phone call. One phone call does it all, one phone call gets it all. And before you know it, we come up with "One call, that's all."

Glen Lerner's tagline—"In a wreck? Need a check?"—is also simple and short, and it implies that Lerner and Rowe Injury Attorneys represents victims of auto accidents. It's memorable because it rhymes, and it can be applied to outdoor advertisements or radio and TV ads very effectively.

What you don't want to do is use a tagline everyone else uses. Things like "Accidents happen," "We can help," or "No fee until we win" are common phrases used by law firms across the country. When you want to stand out, you have to say something different.

Let's take a look at some other tantalizing taglines:

- In Las Vegas, Edward M. Bernstein & Associates tells you, "Enough said, call Ed!"

- Wisconsin's Spencer & Associates LLC says you can "Change Your Pain to Rain."
- Mayberry Law Firm in Florida highlights how hard they work with "Busting Ours to Save Yours."
- Arnold & Smith in North Carolina shows that they're on your side with their tagline: "When it is time to fight, we fight to win."
- Though not a personal injury firm, Vermont's Bauer Gravel Farnham uses "Large firm experience, small firm accessibility" to showcase both their expertise and great client experience.

So, how can you create a great tagline?

First, determine your USP. Then, consider which aspect of that USP can be distilled into a catchy phrase or sentence to make you even more memorable. Finally, do a quick search and make sure no one else is using your tagline (or, at the very least, no one in your state or market).

Take the time to identify what makes you unique, then use your tagline to shout it from the rooftops.

BEING UNIQUE MEANS YOU'RE NOT FOR EVERYONE

It's important to note that the way you position yourself, the way you help clients choose you, will mean that you're right for certain people but wrong for others. Marketing is not about attracting everyone; it's about helping the right people find you—and weeding out the wrong ones.

After all, when you spend those advertising dollars, you want to bring in the best clients for your firm—and you want to be the best fit for them.

Put yourself in the consumer's mindset. If you get into a car accident and just have some whiplash, but not a serious injury, you likely want the most convenient attorney. You understand that you're not looking at a huge case settlement, but you want to make it easy for yourself and get some money to pay for your injuries. In that scenario, you don't need a sledgehammer of an attorney; you just need to get it done.

Now imagine another scenario: your sister loses a leg due to negligence. You're not as worried about convenience anymore; you want justice. You may even want revenge. The people responsible for letting this happen to her need to *pay*. In this case, you don't care where they're located or how far you have to drive to see them; you just want the best person for the job.

The same personal injury firm is probably not going to get both cases, the quick/local/convenient settlement *and* the big-money justice case. Which type of consumer are you trying to reach? Which of those people do you want to help? That answer will give you an idea of the best way to get in front of those people. If it's the first scenario, you might meet the person at the hospital or do everything online so the client doesn't have to go anywhere. If it's the second scenario, you might tell them how you've gotten the highest awards or that you specialize in exactly this type of case, specifying how much you've won for other people in similar situations.

Another way you can stand out is by figuring out exactly what your market needs and then giving it to them. But to do that, you need to know your audience, which is why we'll talk about targeting next.

Additional Personal Injury Mastermind *podcast episodes to check out for more information on differentiation and positioning include:*

- *Episode 80, featuring Mike Papantonio of Levin Papantonio— "Doing Well by Doing Good"*
- *Episode 82, featuring Dave Thomas of Law Tigers—"The Universal Power of Niche"*
- *Episode 83, featuring Seth Godin of Akimbo—"Differentiation: How to Make Your Law Firm a Purple Cow"*

3

YOU CAN'T HIT A BULL'S-EYE IF YOU DON'T KNOW WHERE THE TARGET IS

"I was the first lawyer in America
to advertise on Univision."

–ANGEL REYES OF REYES BROWNE LAW
Personal Injury Mastermind podcast episode 242

AS I'VE SAID, ALL ADVERTISING WORKS; SOME APPROACHES are just more effective than others. The *most* effective way to advertise is to go where your consumers congregate. Anywhere their attention lies is an opportunity for advertising.

But attention changes, and now we're playing a game of attention arbitrage to maximize advertising spend where those prospective clients congregate. How can we get the most attention for the lowest cost?

In the past, people had to use the yellow pages to look up a phone number—that directory had their attention, so it was a good place to advertise. From there, everyone used *TV Guide* to see what was showing that night, so that became the better place to get in front of consumers. Then it moved to TV, advertising via all those commercials that interrupted shows every seven or eight minutes. Commercial advertising helped some of the biggest firms grow, because they took advantage of this form of mass distribution.

Now, people are shifting away from live, broadcast TV with commercials and toward streaming, which offers another opportunity to advertise. Additionally, almost everyone is on social media, so that's another way to get in front of your target audience. We don't know where people will congregate in the future, but if you can get your name in front of those people, you have an opportunity to stand out. If the metaverse ends up taking off, you might be the first personal injury firm to advertise in virtual reality!

The trouble with attention becoming more (or even predominantly) digital is that attention has fractured. Are people watching Netflix, Hulu, Disney+, or Apple TV? What's going to be the next big social media network? Will the metaverse get bigger, or will "the next big thing" be something else we haven't even thought of yet?

Attention will certainly shift again; still, we can make some predictions about where it may go. For example, right now the dominant search engine is Google, but if Microsoft and ChatGPT take market share from Google? Well, then we'll need to shift advertising dollars to Microsoft's side of the street, because that's where the attention will be.

As attention shifts, you have to be the first one into a new market or channel. Be willing to innovate and experiment with what works so that you continue capturing the attention of your prospective clients—and ensure they know who you are.

While some advertising channels have shifted over the years, others have remained fairly consistent. Billboards (and some other traditional forms of advertising) continue to be effective: people still use cars to get around, so putting your face on a busy highway remains a viable strategy. It's stood the test of time, but the competition, value, and cost have increased—because we're all playing the game of attention arbitrage.

Here's the thing: wherever attention moves, that's where you have to be. You need to figure out where your people congregate, because *that's where they are*. You don't want to just fire your message everywhere blindly and hope it finds the right people. Advertising in the PI space is so costly that you have to maximize your ad spend—and the less you spend to get attention, the better.

And in order to get the most attention for your spend and maximize your advertising budget, you have to target that advertising effectively. Targeting starts with knowing who your ideal client is.

CREATE AN AVATAR
(NO, NOT LIKE THE MOVIE WHERE THE GUY PLUGS HIS PONYTAIL INTO A FLYING HORSE)

In order to market effectively, you have to know who you are marketing to. The first step is to create your ideal customer avatar.

If you could design the absolutely perfect client for yourself or your firm, who would that person be? Envision a specific person, even giving your avatar a name to make it more real. It's not "this avatar"; it's John Smith. Are they male or female? Where do they work? What do they do for fun? Where do they hang out? We'll look at more questions to consider in just a moment.

As you begin, it may feel like you're stereotyping, trying to distill all your potential clients down to this one person for your avatar, but try to think of it as the absolutely ideal person to become your client. Think of them as a real person, not a stereotype. What do they need?

The longer you work with clients and the more data you collect, the more refined your avatar will become. Be as specific as you can with the details you have, but it's okay to include some generalities. For example, it's fine to give a range "between the ages of forty and fifty," but not "anyone from ages eighteen to 118." Similarly, you may say, "They generally watch these shows," but you don't want to say, "They watch all the shows and listen to every podcast and radio station." Casting a wider net by including more options might seem positive, but how are you going to advertise everywhere, to everyone? It's impossible!

When creating your avatar, you want to establish the four types of market segmentation:

1. Demographics
2. Geographics
3. Psychographics
4. Behavior

You may not need this fourth area of segmentation, behavior, which asks questions such as "What are their spending habits?" Spending and purchasing habits may not apply, because people don't typically plan to be in a personal injury or auto accident. One important thing to note about behavior, however, is customer loyalty, which may lead to referrals in the future.

GOAT QUOTE

In episode 153 of the *Personal Injury Mastermind* podcast, Jordan Ostroff says, "Demographics is who, geographic is where, psychographic is why—why does someone need you? Why does someone want to hire you? What is the mental stuff that's going to impact them?"

Let's look at some questions to answer as they relate to the first three areas of market segmentation.

Who?

First, look at their demographics:

- What age are they?
- What is their occupation and income?
- What is their race?
- What is their marital status?
- What is their education level?

Where?

Some questions related to geographics would be:

- Where are they located? In what city?
- How far are they from your headquarters?
- What is the primary language they speak?

Why?

Finally, consider the psychographics of your avatar. Psychographics include your avatar's interests, values, and lifestyle. This is the most important area to understand, because it shows how you can help your target customer. Relevant questions include:

- What do they want? What do they need?

- What are their hobbies?
- Where do they hang out?
- What are their interests?
- What are their goals and values?
- What are their pain points? (You're not trying to solve pain points in their daily life; you're solving problems related to whatever personal injury they experienced. How can you help them from that standpoint?)

To give you an idea of what this process looks like in practice, let's create a hypothetical avatar who, in general terms, would capture the ideal family-oriented client for a law firm specializing in auto accidents.

This avatar's name is Frank Jones. He is male, thirty-eight years old, and married with two kids, ages eight and twelve. Frank lives in Detroit, Michigan, and works as a construction laborer making $52,000 a year. He has a high school diploma, doesn't read much, and doesn't attend conferences or visit blogs or websites, but he listens to Joe Rogan's podcast and watches sports. Frank drives a Ford truck to work.

Frank is a family man who works hard and is a good provider. His daughter runs cross-country, and he attends all her meets; he takes his son fishing. The whole family likes to go to football games, where they paint their faces and cheer for the Detroit Lions. Frank is relatively low-tech; having the latest iPhone is not a priority for him.

Frank gets into a car accident on his way to work, totaling his truck. He's worried—he has a physically demanding job, and he doesn't have a disability policy, so he needs to know that he'll be able to continue earning money. His wife is concerned about whether they've saved enough to support the family if Frank needs to take time off and replace his vehicle. Frank's priorities are with taking care of his family, getting his truck paid for, and getting back to work as soon as he can. He wants to avoid adding more bills wherever he can, so he's not going to go to a doctor (or the ER) unless something's really wrong. In terms of hiring an attorney, he doesn't care as much about where they went to school as he does about convenience and their ability to get him enough money to replace his truck—and quickly, because the bills are piling up.

If this were your ideal client avatar and you wanted to choose a USP to appeal to Frank Jones, you would want to highlight convenience: "We come to you, wherever you are" or "Give us a call and we'll handle everything over the phone—you don't even need to come into the office!" Even more importantly, he wants to see: "You don't pay until we win."

If your differentiator is customer experience, you might stand out to Frank if you can provide him with a vehicle until he gets the money to replace his. He may feel more comfortable with a firm that also specializes in construction; if that's one of your niches, be sure to talk up that area of your practice.

Frank likely won't do a lot of deep research on attorneys. If he sees a memorable billboard, he may remember and search for "The Hammer," rather than looking through law firm names.

Because you know this ideal customer avatar—because you know *him*—you know what he wants. Now, it's just a matter of giving it to him, highlighting how convenient it is to work with you, how fast you can get his money and get his car paid for so he can get back to work. All of this information will tell Frank that your firm is the right one for him.

IF YOU ADVERTISE IN A FOREST AND NO ONE IS AROUND TO SEE IT…

Once you know who your avatar is and where they are likely to be found, you want to put your message out there in front of them. The best marketing appeals to your specific, ideal customer.

For Frank Jones, in the previous example, that would mean memorable advertisements on billboards or podcasts—and even during football games or other sporting events. Sports radio is a great place to advertise because construction workers listen to it on the job. On your website, highlight how convenient your firm can make his experience and that he doesn't have to pay anything up front. If he performs a Google search for "Detroit car accident lawyer," you want to make sure your firm appears first on the list of search results. This particular avatar is probably not prevalent on TikTok or Pinterest, so those are some examples of where advertising would be less effective.

Niching can help with targeting as well, because it is easier to reach your avatar in a niche of personal injury law. For example, if you specialize in nursing-home abuse, you would advertise near nursing homes or places where older people and their loved ones might visit. If you focus on trucking, you'd advertise on interstate billboards and with trucking safety divisions. If you specialize in motorcycle accidents, like Law Tigers for example, you would want to build relationships with Harley-Davidson dealers or appear at biker events. That's a select group; they congregate together—and that's where you need to advertise. Grassroots marketing is very effective for motorcycle accident cases, because bikers like to do business with people they know who are like themselves.

GOAT QUOTE

Dave Thomas of Law Tigers says, "Obviously, we have a targeted niche that's just motorcycle cases, and the majority of us are riders ourselves. We approach that if you trust being authentic and being in the trenches with the riders, then the result of that is the trust takes us to the next step of them reaching out to us if they have a need, if they were in an unfortunate accident."

Law Tigers wouldn't necessarily care about marketing to Frank Jones, because he's not their target audience. Similarly, Joe Fried, the trucking accident expert, isn't going to spend his marketing dollars trying to appeal to Frank either. There may be some overlap—his truck driver avatar may also listen to Joe Rogan and watch sports—but he's not specifically targeting family men who are in the construction business and looking for a speedy settlement.

James Farrin and Glen Lerner both say that you have to saturate the market and be one of the top three spenders for your audience to remember you. Because there are so many personal injury attorneys out there, it's much easier and less expensive to saturate a smaller market, in a niched specialty—you're not trying to stand out among so many attorneys or to appeal to so much of the market. You want to maximize your dollars compared to your competitors, which creates an advantage.

Now, just because you focus on one avatar or area of personal injury law, that doesn't mean you're eliminating or automatically saying no to anyone else who might come to you from a different area. If you specialize in motorcycle accidents but someone comes to you after a car accident, you still have the option to say yes to that person—or to refer them to another attorney or firm (who may then refer their motorcycle accident cases to you). The point is that you don't want to try to market to everyone; you want to build relationships with your ideal clients.

You may choose to have multiple avatars and segment your market to reach them in different places. Let's say you create a secondary avatar, a female named Jane Doe. Jane is a stay-at-home mom who takes her kids to school in the morning and picks them up in the afternoon, but otherwise, she is at home. If she also gets into an auto accident, marketing is less likely to reach her in the same places as Frank Jones. She's less interested in sports, but she watches daytime television; therefore, you might advertise on the Hallmark Channel or even your local CBS affiliate.

When you target well, you will appeal to your audience because they'll sense you're *like* them, that you understand who they are and what they need, especially as they are going through a difficult time that caused them to look for a personal injury lawyer. If you know what appeals to them, you can get in front of them *before* they need your services. Then, if and when the time comes, they'll remember that lawyer with the funny billboard or who offers to come to their house, who speaks Spanish, or who dresses like Barbie.

THINGS CHANGE; PEOPLE DO, TOO

Your avatar will likely change over time, as consumer behavior changes over time. If you're still advertising in the yellow pages, Frank Jones is never going to see it. (On the other hand, that would have been the first place Frank's dad looked.) If you currently advertise on social media, you know that more of the older generation uses Facebook, while the younger generations use TikTok and maybe Instagram (at least as of the writing of this book—in a decade, the "kids today" might think only old people know how to Floss or Gritty).

Your avatar may remain very similar, but where you market may change because your target avatar will congregate in different locations over time. You want to remain current, understand your ideal customer, and change your advertising based on their evolving behaviors.

The bigger your firm gets, the more data will influence your marketing decisions—things like which practice areas to target, which locations, where your avatar congregates, and the types or values of cases. If you're a new firm and you're very data-oriented from the beginning, it will serve you even better as you get more volume in the future.

In addition to knowing *who* your avatar is and *where* to reach them, it's important to know *how to talk to them effectively*. That's where your marketing messaging comes in—and that's the topic of chapter 4.

4

WORDS ARE HARD

"Whenever you want people to do something, get them to micro-commit before they do it. So, if they say yes, they'll do it, now they have to follow through—and that first ask is much easier."

–SAM MOLLAEI OF LEGAL FUNNEL
Personal Injury Mastermind podcast episode 121

N EXT TIME YOU'RE DRIVING AROUND TOWN, PAY attention to the billboards you see, particularly those for personal injury attorneys.

You'll likely see a ton of billboards (maybe even your own!) that say things like:

- "INJURED?"
- "HURT?"

- "CAR WRECK?"
- "IN AN ACCIDENT?"
- "¿LESIONADO?"

When I started looking into these kinds of billboards for this chapter, about 90 percent of what I saw used some version of those questions, followed by a firm name and phone number. These billboards, and others like them, basically say, "Congratulations on your family's death and/or dismemberment—now let's get you *paid!*"

Compare those to some of these funny and unique billboard ads:

- Frank Azar's billboard shows a wrecked car and reads, "$545 thousand reasons to call Frank Azar." Underneath, for added memorability, it includes his nickname: "The Strong Arm."
- Davis W. Smith's ad does start with "Injured?" However, he follows up with "Get the gorilla!" and the website GorillaLawFirm.com.
- Robert (Tito) Meyer poses with his dogs and says, "Trust Me, I'm a Lawyer! (My Dogs Do)."

As you can see, personal injury billboards don't *have* to be repetitive or cookie-cutter. So, if you're guilty of leading with "INJURED?" on your billboards, this chapter is for you.

YOUR MESSAGE IS WHAT
YOU SAY ABOUT YOURSELF

I'm not exaggerating when I say that I could print hundreds of pages of billboards, all from different firms, that just say "INJURED?" with a name and phone number. Many of these attorneys are effective enough at a basic level (in that drivers are looking at them, at least once), but they're not *creative*. Their messaging is simply not memorable—and you *must* be memorable in order to stand out from every other personal injury attorney in this crowded field.

But you can't stand out when you're doing the same thing everyone else does, in the same place everyone else does it. If there are forty billboards in the city from eight different firms and they all say some variation of "INJURED?" on them, then they all run together. On the other hand, if you owned thirty-five of those billboards, then the basic "INJURED?" ad with your firm name probably *would* work, simply due to the power of consistency and repetition.

Part of why you hear even the most prominent attorneys say that you need to saturate a market is because their offer isn't different or unique enough to stand out. If you only say "ACCIDENT?" on every billboard, someone would have to see it ten thousand times before remembering your name. But if you show yourself holding a sledgehammer and running toward a semi-truck, they likely only need to see that once or twice to remember The Texas

Hammer. That ad is memorable, funny, and shows Jim Adler's authority. Similarly, John Morgan's messaging is effective because he makes great use of humor. His billboards have included the tagline "Size Matters," his face in a hundred-dollar bill, and him dressed as Santa Claus, saying, "Grandma run over by a reindeer?" Think of Jamie Dimon using explosions in his Super Bowl commercial or Darryl Isaacs, The Kentucky Hammer, who gets on a spaceship and throws a magical hammer at enemies, evoking the Marvel Cinematic Universe. Their messages are funny and entertaining, but most importantly, they *stand out* and are *memorable*.

You want to be known. You want prospective clients to like and trust you, so they want to hire you. But first you have to get their attention, and to do that, you need to tell them about yourself in an entertaining, memorable, and authentic way.

You do that through your *messaging*.

Legal marketing expert Harlan Schillinger has a saying: "You get what you ask for." It's simple, but powerful. If you're asking for truck accidents, you're more likely to receive them.

You can use different forms of messaging to appeal to clients at different stages of the sales funnel. The three stages of the funnel (top, middle, and bottom) directly correlate to the three parts of the most important principle in marketing: your clients must know, like, and trust you. At the top of the funnel, people are getting to know you; in the middle, you want them to start to like you; by the bottom, they need to trust you if they are going to hire you.

Getting to Know You

At the top of the funnel, you are garnering awareness, so you need easy-to-consume information that appeals to a broad audience. Gary Vaynerchuk exemplifies this approach with his content on happiness—who doesn't want to be happier? This top-of-the-funnel messaging is content that reaffirms what people already believe and know to be true.

I see many personal injury attorneys run into a problem at this stage when, instead of helping people gain awareness of their existence, they promote their business with posts about the steps to take after getting into a car accident. You could make a strong argument that those attorneys have it backward: instead of posting about injuries and accidents in the hope that people will remember those posts when they need a lawyer, their posts should be about getting to know that attorney or firm—for something *other than personal injury law*. That way, if one of their followers does have an accident, they already know this attorney. Mike Morse, for example, has gained success on social media by reviewing pizza places. Everyone likes pizza! Other attorneys use humor or feel-good anecdotes.

Whatever specific tactic you take, make sure your messaging perspective:

- Is easy to consume
- Appeals to a broad audience

Getting to Like You

If the top of the funnel is about getting to *know* you, the middle of the funnel is about helping your audience *like* you. At this stage, they are forming an opinion about you, so you want your messaging to focus on connection and emotion. After all, they can know who you are, but if they don't like you, they're not going to work with you.

Darryl Isaacs is particularly good at this part of the funnel. His social media includes pictures and videos of him helping dogs get adopted through the Humane Society, going to the grocery store and showing the snacks he loves—even dyeing eggs at Easter!

> *Ed Herman of Brown & Crouppen calls this stage "brand love." To hear more about his viral marketing techniques, check out episode 14 of the* Personal Injury Mastermind *podcast.*

When you're trying to develop a connection and get your audience to have a positive opinion of you, you want to show yourself to be:

- Likable
- Humble and/or self-deprecating

- Approachable
- Trustworthy

Trust Me

Finally, the bottom of the funnel is transactional; this is where you can make the hard ask for the target to consider hiring you when they need an attorney. Remember Lerner and Rowe's tagline: "In a Wreck? Need a Check?" That's right in your face about how working with them can be lucrative for you.

You need two ways of standing out to approach this stage of your messaging:

- A unique selling proposition about how you're different and why they should work with you (Don't know what I'm talking about? Go back and reread chapter 3!)
- A personal injury niche (for example, specializing in trucking accidents, highlighting that your firm is woman-owned, or even portraying yourself as the biggest Philly sports fan)

By the bottom of the funnel, you are no longer speaking to everyone; your messaging at this stage should specifically target your avatar.

GOAT QUOTE

Matthew Dolman, president and managing partner of Dolman Law Group, joined me on episode 162 of the *Personal Injury Mastermind* podcast to talk about how to highlight expertise:

> If I'm going to put together a proper profile to… illustrate my experience, authoritativeness, and trustworthiness behind my name and behind my law firm's name, well, I want to highlight what is my experience in practicing law. So, "Matt Dolman's been practicing"—and I hate talking about myself in third person—"for twenty years, been licensed in the state of Florida, he's handled X amount of cases." If you want to say you are board-certified or you're a member of the Million Dollar Advocates Forum or you were selected Legal Elite—whatever awards that you could put there that will actually show that you are an expert and trusted by others in your field, let alone you should be trusted by consumers.

THE PSYCHOLOGY OF PERSUASION

There are psychological reasons why people make buying and hiring decisions. Thus, you can use different forms of psychology to persuade people to buy from you or use your services.

You Scratch My Back

The first tactic is called reciprocity. When you build up relationship currency—meaning you pay something, like information or advice, into the relationship—the other person feels like they owe you something in return. That's reciprocity. They feel inclined, almost obligated, to work with you in the future.

Consider sharing valuable information on social media or your podcast—or being a contributing member of the community. Grassroots charity-based marketing initiatives, like turkey drives or backpack giveaways, *are* content. Even though you're doing something tangible, when you utilize your action for your social media it becomes messaging. You're saying, "I'm a good person, and I've got your back."

Reciprocity shines in personal injury. This is a good reason to highlight having free consultations or your policy of "no fees unless we win." A free consultation is a form of reciprocity—you give your time, attention, and expertise to the prospective client, for nothing. In return, they can do you a favor by hiring you to represent them and help them achieve the best possible outcome for their case.

PERSONAL INJURY LAWYER MARKETING

Play It Again, Sam

Having a consistent message makes you more memorable. This is why TV advertisers advise saturating a channel—that repetition forms memorability.

People Can Be Lemmings

Social proof is a powerful form of marketing. People expect you to say that you're the best attorney, but when *someone else* says you're the best, their reputation validates that statement. Social proof can include video testimonials, client reviews, case results, awards—anything compelling that specifically fits your narrative, the story you're trying to tell about yourself and how your firm can help them.

> *In most markets, you can't call yourself the best—but you can say that someone else thinks you're the best or has voted you the best.*

Respect My Authoritah!

The next tactic is to show that you are an authority. This is different from social proof—social proof shows that you can do something; being an authority means that you are *the best* at it. Authority includes authoring a particular type of case law, speaking at events, highlighting the size of your business, and having your face on billboards and TV commercials. Billboards and TV ads are expensive, so when people see you on them, they're inclined to think you must be legit.

Authority also comes from receiving out-of-state referrals, particularly among your peers. Highlighting high-dollar case results or specific expertise can help demonstrate your authority to clients and colleagues alike.

Be Life Cereal—Mikey Likes It!

Likability means that you are approachable. Many criminal defense attorneys pose with scowls on their faces and say, "We'll fight for you" or "We'll murder the competition." That aggressive demeanor may work in that area of the law, but clients in the personal injury space are frequently looking for someone approachable or relatable, because they are in a very vulnerable place, often going through one of the worst periods of their lives.

Being approachable encourages clients to like you—and is itself a method of persuasion. This is where videos can really shine. Pictures of you smiling are also good, but it doesn't always have to be warm and fuzzy. If you're the top attorney for traumatic brain injuries, you may want to portray yourself as the person who will rip the insurance company a new one.

The Most Wonderful Thing about Tiggers Is I'm the Only One

Scarcity is another form of psychological persuasion. This could be geographic exclusivity, the hours you're available, or even time constraints. Mass torts, for example, have a statute of limitations—that creates a time constraint.

Scarcity can also come from being one of the only practitioners in your niche. If you are the only knee-joint litigator, the only one who speaks Spanish in your market, or the only woman-owned firm in your city, then you can create that sense of scarcity to help you stand out.

> *Want to read more about this topic? Check out Robert B. Cialdini's book* Influence: The Psychology of Persuasion.

Act Now! Operators Are Standing By

Once you've persuaded them, people need to be told what to do. Every message needs a call to action. What's your ask?

Typically, there are two types of asks: you're trying to either sell something or expand your following. Posting on social media and asking people to comment, subscribe, like, and share are engagement-based calls to action. Engagement-based calls to action help with your awareness, reach, and distribution.

A transactional call to action, on the other hand, is when you say, "Contact us if you've been hurt" or "If you need an attorney, call now." These transactional calls to action are heavier, so in most situations you want to use more engagement-based calls to action than transactional ones.

COPYWRITING TIPS AND TRICKS

Here are some additional tips to utilize in your messaging:

Highlight your unique selling proposition. Showing prospective clients why your firm is different from others out there will help you stand out.

Apply humor, if possible, for virality and likability. Humor can also make you more memorable.

You can be entertaining, without just going for laughs, by being awesome: Russell Nicolet bought a Super Bowl commercial just to jam on the guitar. The next year, he busted out a sick rap. You don't expect an attorney to do *either* of those things. His YouTube video alone got forty-eight thousand views—not to mention the millions of people who watched the Super Bowl (and commercials!). His commercials are memorable because he did something cool and different.

At the middle and bottom of the funnel, speak directly to your avatar—particularly their demographics, geographics, and psychographics. Create messaging that centers on solutions for their specific problems or pains.

Limit the use of legalese. Make your content easy to digest for your prospective client.

Try to create an emotional connection, through storytelling when possible. Merry Fountain got hit by a car and suffered severe injuries while cycling. She chose a niche in bicycle advertising. Being a bicyclist herself, she's already a member of bike-riding associations, where she can talk about safety and wearing helmets. She uses her story, which is powerful, is memorable, and encourages a personal and emotional connection.

Finally, lead with empathy. Because you are a personal injury attorney, most of your clients and prospective clients are hurt or in pain. As we saw at the beginning of the chapter, many billboards come across like, "Congratulations on getting hurt! Time for a payday." That can be off-putting. No one wants to feel they're cashing in on getting hurt or losing a loved one; that is how the stereotypes of lawyers as bloodsuckers and ambulance chasers were born. Those messages are dehumanizing (both to your clients and yourself). Instead, you need to come across as genuine and caring.

Your messaging is an important piece of the marketing puzzle—but it's just one piece, and you have to use every tool in your toolbox to beat the competition. In the next chapter, we'll look at how to leverage your unique advantages to be the best.

USE IT OR LOSE IT

"If you're not being tech-competent, and not understanding how you can be more efficient, you're stealing from your client."

–PRATIK SHAH OF ESQUIRETEK
Personal Injury Mastermind podcast episode 101

L EVERAGE HAS MANY DEFINITIONS:

- The exertion of force by means of a lever or an object used in the manner of a lever
- The increase in force gained by using a lever
- The use of a lever to maximum advantage

These are all definitions as related to physics, but you may be more familiar with leverage in terms of the ability to borrow and increase the use of capital for real estate. I want to focus on one definition as it relates to a personal injury law firm:

- The influence of power used to achieve a desired result

If you consider your business to be in competition (and as a personal injury attorney, you certainly should), leverage offers the strategy to win. Your competitive edge will allow you to get a leg up on your competitors.

Specifically, let's look at four areas of leverage you can use to *your* maximum advantage: labor, capital, technology, and content.

> *Entrepreneur and investor Naval Ravikant calls these areas of leverage the four Cs: collaboration, capital, code, and content.*

HOW TO MOVE A PILE OF ROCKS

The first kind of leverage that can give you an advantage over your competition is labor.

Consider the age-old example of leveraging labor: Imagine you have a pile of rocks in one place that you need moved to another place. Instead of one individual moving each rock, one at a time, which is tedious and time-consuming, you can enlist more people to move more rocks at the *same* time, thereby completing the task faster and more efficiently.

We all know that, over time, we need to hire more people. We only have so much time and can only personally do so many things. Having more people working for you can yield an advantage based on the amount of output, power, and force available in your business. This labor can benefit all areas of your business: marketing, social media, sales, intake, etc. For example, with more people, you may be able to have an intake team that answers calls 24/7, not just during the normal 9-to-5 business hours, or you could hire intake team members who are bilingual. If your competition's intake team only speaks English, and yours can help clients in English *and* Spanish, you have a leveraged advantage. You may even be able to hire additional attorneys, which means fewer open cases.

GOAT QUOTE

In episode 219 of the *Personal Injury Mastermind* podcast, Daniel Morgan of Morgan & Morgan talks about the importance of answering every call quickly, using a process his uncle developed with the motto "Hook it and book it":

We have a firm policy that...if there's more than thirty seconds to a minute queue and that person hangs up, most likely, they're not hanging up and calling back in thirty minutes when the queue times are bad. Most likely, they're hanging up and going to the next line on Google or the next recommendation they got from their Facebook friends.

The whole hook-it-and-book-it philosophy is really, one, if you're hanging up on the client or if you're saying, "Hey, I think this might be a case. We'll call you back in thirty minutes and let you know," most likely, that client's gone forever...It'd be like you're deep-sea fishing and you pull in a marlin, and right before it gets to the bow, you say, "You know what? I'm going to unhook that. I'll catch that same fish in about thirty minutes from now," and go from there. Now, once you get that fish off the hook, it's gone forever. It's the same in catching cases. It is all 24/7.

The one disclaimer here is that, typically, your highest cost walks on two legs, so you need to be aware of the amount you're earning per full-time employee. As of the writing of this book in 2024, a general rule of thumb that lends itself to profitability is that each employee needs to generate at least $200,000 in revenue. (Thus, if you have twenty employees, you should be grossing at least $4 million in business.) Obviously, the higher the number, the better.

The real game to play, however, is the game of arbitrage—how much you pay compared to your competitors. Pricing arbitrage can come in many different forms. For example, due to technological advances, you don't have to hire people who live in a specific location. You may be able to hire an employee based in the Midwest for less than one who lives on the West Coast—for the same job.

This concept expands with your willingness to use international arbitrage, where there can be significant discounts in what you pay people in other countries, based on the output they produce. Some law firms prefer US-based labor, because they think the skills are better than international labor—but what if the international labor were just as talented and communicated just as well, for a fraction of the cost? If it costs one-tenth as much, you could hire ten international employees versus one full-time employee in the US. This does not mean you shouldn't hire American employees; I'm just highlighting the true advantages of your dollar as it relates to labor.

In chapter 7, we'll also cover in-house labor versus outsourcing, because there are some tasks and situations for which you don't need a full-time employee.

In this chapter, I'm going to give you lists of Personal Injury Mastermind *podcast episodes you can listen to for additional examples of leverage in action.*

For more information as it relates to labor, check out episode 52, featuring Chris Mursau of Topgrading, Inc.—"Hiring for Excellence, Interview Strategy, and the New PIP."

MONEY MAKES THE WORLD GO 'ROUND

Capital comes in many forms, and it allows you to leverage the advantage of your buying power.

One way to do so is through your merchant services and credit card processing fees. Typically, the higher amount you earn (and therefore the more you're processing), the lower your transaction fees can be.

But that's just one example, purely from a finance/administrative perspective. You can also negotiate your lease if you choose to have a brick-and-mortar location; on the other hand, operating a remote company can also offer a distinct capital advantage.

GOAT QUOTE

On episode 209 of *Personal Injury Mastermind*, Jack Zinda shares his approach to capitalization:

> On the capitalization side, you've got to know your numbers first, so you need to know, "What is my average time to resolve a case? How much do I resolve a case for, and how much does it cost to acquire a case?" So with that information, you can plug that in and figure out, "Okay, what's my start-up capital needs, office space, marketing dollars, people on the ground? When am I going to get my first case, and how long until I'm going to monetize it?" We went really light on the overhead at first. We worked in virtual offices, had one attorney, had all our staff in Austin before we started adding a lot of people to different spots.

Another way to leverage capital is through consolidation to create more efficiencies. For example, Andrew Finkelstein of Finkelstein & Partners also owns Jacoby & Meyers, Diller Law, and a few other firms—but on the back end, they all share one administrative department, HR department, and financial team. It is a capital advantage to only pay to operate one of each of these departments, which can then serve multiple firms.

There are also opportunities for capital advantages relating to economies of scale. Most people are looking for a 10 percent return, ideally. But what if you prepaid your marketing up front, for a discount? Most businesses will supply you with at least a 10 percent discount in exchange for prepayment. Another example would be buying marketing packages in serious bulk. If, for example, you buy one billboard, it'll cost X dollars, but if you buy a thousand billboards, it's not going to cost you 1,000X; it will be some percentage lower. We also see this principle as it relates to TV spots, Google Ads, and pay-per-click: the more you purchase, the lower the cost per impression can be.

Most personal injury firms find it challenging to use this type of leverage because they don't reach economies of scale on a high enough spend to get the lowest cost per acquisition. Additionally, they tend to target an overly small geographic area. If you're a Houston personal injury law firm and you just bid for pay-per-click around Houston, you're bidding against everyone, because they're all focused on that market. But what would it look like if you bid on the entire state of Texas, to get cases cheaper in certain areas? Or expand that: What if you bid on cases throughout the entire United States? How much cheaper would your cost per case be versus focusing on a smaller central location where more saturation occurs?

Another form of capital advantage is cash flow and borrowing capabilities. In some cases you try, you may not see a return on your capital for many years. Firms that can finance their own cases have an advantage over those that aren't capitalized. Most personal injury firms take auto accident cases because those cases tend to settle frequently and quickly, especially as compared to a mass tort that may take several years to pay out.

A note of caution as it relates to undercapitalization: do not move into a new market if you are undercapitalized, because when you do, you have to saturate that market in order to be remembered, known, and seen. If you don't have enough capital to do so, you're just wasting your money and your time.

GOAT QUOTE

In episode 84 of the *Personal Injury Marketing Mastermind* podcast, Glen Lerner of Lerner and Rowe says, "There's some incredibly competitive markets that are just so skewed they don't even make sense. If you're not going to spend enough to be [one of] the top four or five players in the market, I just think it's almost better to find another way to advertise, find a niche where you can have a strong presence."

A final aspect of capital you can leverage is your ability to persevere through unforeseen circumstances. For example, during the height of the COVID-19 pandemic, when many businesses were closed and people weren't driving much, there were far fewer auto accidents. Firms with a capital advantage could continue to expand with *less* competition because people pulled out and didn't market during that time period.

> In addition to the episodes previously mentioned, Personal Injury Mastermind *episodes covering leveraged capital include episode 122, featuring Andrew Finkelstein of Finkelstein & Partners—"Financial Security: How to Build Long-Term Wealth."*

THE FUTURE IS HERE

To understand the importance of leveraging technology to your advantage, just ask yourself: Are you farming without a tractor? Would you go row by row, harvesting crops by hand? Of course not! It's the same in the legal field—there's leverage in technology if you look for it, become aware of it, and are receptive to it. A lot of it is emerging and new, but it can stand as a significant advantage if you're more willing (or at least more willing than your competition) to adapt and try different innovations.

If you're not willing to adapt, hire from the younger generations that are more accustomed to the use of technology. They can serve as a buffer between the technology and you—and your firm still reaps the advantages.

Some examples of current (as of the writing of this book) technologies you could consider leveraging:

- **Discovery**: EsquireTek can automate your discoveries, which is a massive time-saver. Again, your highest expense walks on two feet, so if you can use technology to automate a big portion of discovery, that's a huge advantage for you.

- **Demands**: EvenUp uses AI to accelerate the process of generating demands. Their website phrases it well: "Save time, win more, and settle faster."

- **Intake**: CaptureNow automates intake and ensures that every call gets answered right away, day or night, so your clients don't have to wait.

- **Marketing**: Yext aggregates your location; PI firms use it for directory and address dispersion.

- **Review Acquisition**: GatherUp, Birdeye, and Podium can all automate this process.

- **Communication**: Slack, Zoom, and Microsoft Teams are all widely used for a reason.

- **Referrals**: Attorney Share operates a referral marketplace, putting attorneys with referrals to send in contact with attorneys who are actively seeking those kinds of cases.

- **CRMs**: Lead Docket, Clio, Litify, Salesforce, etc. can all leverage technological advantages based on data and transparency.

GOAT QUOTE

Kyle Newman of James Newman, P.C., says, "As a young lawyer, trial tech has been the single greatest asset I've had, to consistently win against much older adversaries."

New and emerging technologies that relate to marketing include ChatGPT and other artificial intelligence, which can be used for content creation. Rather than engaging (and paying) a writer, artificial intelligence offers a tool to enhance your creativity and productivity for a *very* minimal investment of capital.

There are two types of AI. The first is traditional, logic-based AI. Examples include live chat, which consists of a series of if/then responses:

- "Have you been hurt (yes or no)?"
- If the answer is yes, the chatbot goes on to ask, "Tell me about your accident. Was it a car accident or a motorcycle accident?"
    - Motorcycle
- "How many people were involved?"
    - Two
- "What were the ages of the people involved?"
- And so on...

This type of AI follows a strict line of logic, essentially using a response tree.

There's CRM-based AI, operations AI, and project management tools that have AI, but most of these are also logic-based. For example, tools like Intaker and SimplyConvert harness AI-based chat that utilizes logic to see if prospects meet certain criteria and then signs them up, without involving a human being.

The second form of AI is search generative. Generative AI does what it says: it generates the answer based upon machine-learning algorithms that pull unique data and synthesize an original response. It is not a series of if/then statements; it is a tool that generates unique results based upon specific, customized prompts.

Personal Injury Mastermind *episodes covering leverage using technology include:*

- *Episode 2, featuring Jessie Hoerman of SimplyConvert–"Utilizing Chatbots and AI for Law Firms"*
- *Episode 13, featuring Terry Dohrmann of Litify–"Streamlining Practice Management and Revolutionizing Efficiency"*
- *Episode 99, featuring Bob Simon of the Simon Law Group and Justice HQ–"Collaboration before Competition"*
- *Episode 101, featuring Pratik Shah of EsquireTek–"Discovering the Power of Automation"*
- *Episode 120, featuring Anthony Johnson of the Johnson Firm (named the "techiest lawyer" by the American Bar Association)–"Innovation and Disruption: How Tech Is Driving the Legal Industry Forward"*
- *Episode 121, featuring Sam Mollaei of Legal Funnel–"Building Blocks: Create a Virtual, Automated, and Scalable Law Firm"*

- *Episode 138, featuring Kyle Newman of James Newman, P.C.–"How to Win More Cases: Technology in the Courtroom"*

- *Episode 239, featuring Jack Newton of Clio–"Toolkit: Legal Tech, Streamline Legal Marketing, Intake, and Operations"*

BE AN INFLUENCER

You can leverage the number of people you speak to and influence via your content distribution channels to give you an advantage over those who don't have the same reach. As an example, if you have an email list of ten thousand people, versus someone else who only has a thousand people, you have a ten-to-one leveraged advantage—or ten-thousand-to-one against the person who doesn't have an email list at all!

The same is true of social media distribution. How many followers do you have? Someone with hundreds of thousands—or even millions—of Instagram followers has a distinct leveraged advantage, so any content they create has influence and power.

TV advertising has been so popular in past decades because it has massive distribution capabilities. If you are on TV, many more people will see you. The same goes for radio, and now podcasts, where the number of subscribers can be leveraged distribution. The amount of content on your website for search engine optimization (SEO) is another opportunity for leverage: the content earns backlinks naturally, and the traffic itself is a good signal for visibility.

In fact, this form of leverage applies to every channel you can think of: TV, radio, podcasts, SEO, social media, email, billboards, reviews, and media appearances (especially on major outlets that have massive distribution where you are quoted as an expert and can piggyback on their marketing efforts to reach way beyond your own distribution).

Reviews can also be categorized as content for leverage. Firms that are very selective about the number of cases they take, or referral firms that are essentially a marketing department that refers cases out, have disadvantages here because it's more challenging for them to acquire reviews. Settlement firms, on the other hand, generate high volume. If your case selection criteria are not as high, you have a leveraged advantage in the number of cases you'll accept or the number of practice areas you cover, compared to those that do not cover as many cases.

Additionally, if you have a celebrity endorsement or testimonial, you can use that as leverage based on their name recognition compared to that of a generic individual. A firm with access to that celebrity has an advantage over a firm that doesn't.

Major trial victories, especially those that garner headlines, can be leveraged against firms that don't have those big numbers—a client is more likely to sign with you after reading about those big wins because they think they have a better chance of winning.

Personal Injury Mastermind *episodes that discuss lever-aged advantages of content include:*

- *Episode 92, featuring Marc Anidjar of Anidjar & Levine—"The Secret Sauce for Managing and Marketing"*
- *Episode 129, featuring Robert Ingalls of LawPods—"Podcasting for Attorneys: A Crash Course"*
- *Episode 144, featuring Neama Rahmani of West Coast Trial Lawyers—"Omnichannel Marketing: Vision, Execution, and Growth"*
- *Episode 149, featuring Greg Star of Carvertise—"Branded Rideshare Vehicles: Retarget to Quality Leads"*

As you can see, your leverage ties in with your positioning (discussed in chapter 2)—that which helps you stand out also gives you an advantage over your competition.

I am often asked, "Chris, why don't you attend more conferences?" I usually make up a lame excuse, but in reality, it's not worth my time in most instances, given that I can leverage my podcast. If I go to a conference, I am one of many speakers. But staying at home in my office and doing the podcast effectively makes me a keynote speaker every week, to an audience of thousands.

In recent chapters, we've looked at positioning, targeting, messaging, and leverage—all focused on *how* to market. In chapter 6, we'll switch gears and look at *who* is best suited to do your marketing.

6

DIY VS. HIRE A GUY

"You have to let go of the thought that you're
the only one who can do your work."

–LUIS SCOTT, FORMERLY OF BADER SCOTT INJURY LAWYERS
Personal Injury Mastermind podcast episode 106

I MAGINE FOR A MOMENT THAT YOU JUST BOUGHT A BIG, beautiful new house. Out front is a gorgeous expanse of green grass—a perfect oasis.

But nothing remains pristine without care. Now, you're left asking yourself, *Who will maintain my lawn?*

The way I see it, you have three options.

Option one: you can do it yourself. If you've never done this before, you'll have to figure everything out—how often to mow, what lawn mower to use, when to fertilize, and which weed control works best. You'll have to put in the time too. Every Sunday, you'll be out there with the mower and weed eater. You have to water it (or install a sprinkler system—another learning opportunity!). You have to fertilize it, weed it, and do everything else your lawn needs to remain a verdant Eden instead of an eyesore. At the end of the day, you can take pride in a job well done.

Then there's option two: you can pay a neighborhood kid (or your own kid!) twenty bucks to mow the lawn for you. If the kid has their own lawn mower, you don't have to purchase equipment, but you may still need to provide fertilizer or weed killer. You'll likely have to pay extra if you want them to do anything but the basics. And let's be honest; the kid probably does a decent job, but it can be hit or miss whether they'll show up consistently or have something better to do. They might not do the job as well as you could, but hey—time is money, and now your weekends are free.

Finally, we have option three: hire a lawn-care service to do everything for you. They come every week (or even more often when needed), rain or shine. Their dedicated experts have everything they need to keep your lawn looking its best—with nothing more needed from you than to set up a recurring payment. They fertilize when needed, remove pesky weeds, rake the lawn in autumn, and give it some extra water when it gets hot in the summer. Because they are experts at what they do, your curb appeal is greater than ever!

None of these choices is necessarily better or worse than the others; it's all a matter of what will work best for you (and your budget)—and that may change at different stages of your life.

WHO WILL DO THE WORK?

As we know, times have changed as technology has allowed for greater interconnectivity. In the previous chapter's discussion of leverage, I talked about how, in order to move a pile of rocks, you probably just needed to get more people on the job. Now, however, you can use technology to move the rocks for you—with fewer (or, in some cases, no) people involved.

When it comes to professional services, you have to make a decision about how you want to get more labor leverage. When it comes to marketing, you also have a decision to make about what's right for you: using in-house labor, contracting with a freelancer, or hiring an agency to do the job.

That decision comes down to control and effort. Having an in-house marketing employee or team offers high control—but also requires high effort. Utilizing freelance labor tends to involve medium control and effort, and hiring an agency yields lower control but also takes much less effort than either of the previous two options. If you want complete control, hiring your marketing staff in-house would likely suit you best. If, however, you are more willing to delegate and relinquish some control, you could potentially benefit from utilizing freelance talent or hiring an agency.

> *The central premise of the book* Who Not How *by Dan Sullivan is that instead of asking ourselves, "How can I do this?" we should be asking, "Who can do this for me?"*
>
> *If you want to learn to do something yourself, that process is going to be linear and slow—but if you hire someone who already possesses that knowledge, it becomes exponential and fast.*

Most personal injury firms undergo an evolution as they grow. First, they hire a marketing assistant or marketing manager to take over some of the roles and responsibilities. Gradually, a higher level of management experience becomes necessary, at which point they may bring in a director of marketing or CMO. Once the firm grows large enough, they then move some of the disciplines in-house for greater control. I've seen law firms be successful moving marketing in-house as they reach the mid-eight figures or are approaching the nine-figure mark.

As the owner of a law firm, you likely wear multiple hats: legal, administrative, marketing, sales, and business generation from referrals and relationships. How are you supposed to find time to *also* provide oversight to the vendors and freelancers, or even the one or two in-house hires? To get greater usage of your time and essentially multiply yourself, you can start shedding some of those hats by hiring a marketing assistant or manager.

In the highly saturated personal injury space, one of the greatest skills most firm owners can possess is an understanding of marketing and business development. While you don't need to know everything about a particular discipline, you do need to understand who to hire and how to measure their skills.

Let's take a closer look at each of the three options and discuss how you can make the best decision for your needs.

KEEP IT IN-HOUSE

Hiring an employee for in-house marketing is slower and somewhat riskier than hiring a freelancer or agency because you have to find, hire, and train the talent. It also requires more effort—you have to go through a longer hiring process, then you have to train them, then you have to provide oversight in terms of leadership and advancement, and *then* you have to continually keep them happy and in alignment with your culture and core values. Finally, if at any point you decide to part ways with an employee, you will likely then owe them unemployment—a more expensive and involved process than simply ending a contract.

Dunbar's Number states that humans have the capacity to remain connected to a group of about 150 other people. In larger organizations, there's a cap on how many people a leader can manage before requiring the assistance of employees who don't generate revenue, such as HR professionals. Because of the complexities of hiring in-house, even more non-revenue-generating staff becomes necessary as the firm grows. This is another reason why larger, eight- to nine-figure firms gravitate toward hiring in-house once they have these HR and culture employees established to manage people, keep them happy, and make them feel aligned with the vision as part of a community.

The potential upside of hiring in-house is that you have more control. You can hire an employee to do whatever you need them to do. They work for you, which means you can be very specific in tailoring the role to fit your needs. There's also more creativity. You can make your marketing more bespoke, custom-tailoring it to your needs as well.

Keep in mind that not all firms have the same hiring options. Whereas newer law firms may work in a remote capacity, traditional law firms that work in brick-and-mortar locations are constrained to hiring from the talent pool in their geographic location.

GOAT QUOTE

Bill Pintas of Pintas & Mullins was on episode 237 of the *Personal Injury Mastermind* podcast, and he had this to say about in-house marketing:

> We originate all the marketing internally, from pay-per-click [PPC] to TV. I mean, our chief marketing officer has thirty-five years of experience in television

buys. We're very robust on our pay-per-clicks. We've been invited out to Google headquarters twice. They said, "We haven't worked with a law firm that does what you do."

We run a lot of Facebook ads, and we do a lot of other proprietary type[s] of marketing, and we're doing it internally. We're really, really good at it. And so we can originate cases cheaper, because we're not paying an agency fee, and we know what we're doing. And not every case type is good for TV, or PPC, or Facebook, or for other marketing channels, and certain case types work really well with it. And so since we can go ahead and do all of them, we can test one against the other. And we kind of have a pretty good feel for which one works and which one doesn't work.

If you have marketing needs that are not easily repeatable or productized, or if the duties may change, you likely want to hire someone in-house.

The general best practice for hiring a marketing employee in-house is to start by reviewing résumés, but also consider the actual application of the role you're hiring for. If you're hiring an SEO specialist, have them perform a competitive SEO audit. If you're hiring a web designer, ask them to show you some creative work. If you're hiring a Google Ads professional, have them put together a strategic one-page plan on how to build out your Ads campaign. If you're looking for a marketing assistant and one of their core responsibilities will be writing, have them write a blog post or do a written assessment (and, of course, pay them for their time). Because it's so costly to hire, you want them to prove that they can do the work *before* you make a decision; a paid assessment shows that they have the necessary behaviors and skills for the role.

I'm a huge proponent of recording video interviews to aid in recall. When you do a lot of interviews, after a while, they can all blend together. Having them recorded on video also means that you have a historical archive that can act as a future recruiting list.

In addition to checking references of employment, speak with some of their clients if they've done client work or managed previous accounts. What better way to hear how they work than directly from the client's mouth?

Once you have hired, you want to topgrade vigorously. You can make C players into B players, but you typically won't turn a C player into an A player. Remember the age-old saying: hire slowly, fire quickly. Keeping someone on who is not suited for the role is costly and, from a marketing perspective, can have negative ramifications that last in perpetuity for your brand or image.

FIND A FREELANCER

When contracting freelancers, you have the benefit of pricing arbitrage; you can utilize international labor and benefit from different pay rates and expectations. You also don't have to pay freelancers' payroll taxes or offer benefits or insurance. Additionally, you have access to a much wider talent pool, because you are not hiring someone to work in-house at your office.

Unlike with employees, whose sole focus is the job you hired them to do, you will have to bid for freelancers' time. They will do what you want, but they are likely working on multiple projects simultaneously (or, if you want to be their sole project, you'll have to wait for their availability to open up—and likely pay more for the privilege).

It's fairly easy to find freelancers on job boards, where you can review their résumés, experience, and testimonials. You're contracting with a freelancer who knows the craft, so they're advertising their skillset. This makes the decision of who to hire faster than the slow process of hiring in-house. Additionally, while you will need to provide a scope for the project or task you want them to complete, freelancers then complete the task with less oversight than an employee—and none of the required training or team building.

There is also typically less brand risk when hiring a freelancer (or agency). Glassdoor is notorious for receiving negative reviews from candidates who weren't hired, but freelancers and agencies have their own reputations to consider when posting publicly and thus are less likely to threaten potential future opportunities.

Most freelancer websites will have profiles where you can review each individual's experience, tenure, tests or certifications, and often written reviews. This is again a perfect scenario for doing an assessment. If you find a candidate you like, hire them for a specific project and see if you work well with them. Freelancers are typically used to proving their abilities (whereas assessments may be less expected for employees). There are multiple gig-economy marketplaces where these individuals congregate, so it is much easier to find freelancers now than it was in the past.

The most important tip I can share is that, even though they're not compensated with benefits, you should treat freelancers as well as you would treat an employee. Give freelancers the same respect, communication, and community that you would give an in-house person, because the biggest risk from a freelancer is losing them to a higher bidder—but if freelancers are happy with their current gig, they won't be actively looking for another.

PARTNER UP, STRATEGICALLY

Finally, you can hire an agency to run your marketing for you. This option makes sense when you want to give input but ultimately rely on their expertise—you wouldn't tell a chef how to run their kitchen, just as if I got injured and came to you, I wouldn't tell you how to try the case. Essentially, you cede control in favor of having a marketing expert do the work for you. This arrangement frees up your time to focus on what *you* are the expert in—practicing personal injury law. Instead of half-assing multiple things, you can whole-ass exactly what you're good at doing. What are your high-value activities? I'm guessing they don't include SEO or web development, so paying people who do that all day every day means you can focus on having the greatest impact in your firm and for your clients.

Engaging an agency will be faster than hiring someone in-house or contracting with a freelancer. Agencies already know how to perform their craft and provide the service. They will have someone who knows social media—what to post and the right cadence. If you want an agency to perform SEO for your firm, you'll get multiple people—copywriters, link builders, developers, etc.—and utilization pulled from multiple disciplines. If you tried to do the same in-house, it would likely cost a lot more, because one individual isn't suited for all those roles. An agency can provide shared utilization across multiple roles because they have multiple clients, so they can keep each role filled with someone focusing full-time on their area.

One caveat: some agencies operate more like vendors; they are basically operational arms for quantitative actions based upon direction. If you want control and you're looking for quantitative output, you may be able to find these hybrids classified as vendors or operations arms.

> *In his book* The Boutique: How to Start, Scale, and Sell a
> Professional Services Firm, *Greg Alexander drives home
> the point that typically the greatest cost for a firm walks
> on two feet. If you want to move faster and get a better cost,
> that is more likely to happen with a freelancer or agency.*

When hiring an agency, be wary of long-term contracts before that agency has shown proof of work. Month-to-month contracts have to earn their keep every month, so anyone who tries to lock you into a long-term contract without a prior relationship is a red flag. The exception would be for personal injury firms looking for exclusive relationships, where an agency can have clients in other fields but only works with that one personal injury firm—that would be the one case where you're not really exclusive unless it accompanies a long-term contract.

Many personal injury firms' number one request is geographic exclusivity, which is not something they are legally required to have—and this is a bad decision, in most cases, because agencies that freely give geographic exclusivity are often not very good at what they do. Those who understand their value don't want to give that exclusivity.

I'm writing this as an agency owner, and you can ask for references if you want...but am I really going to share a reference who will give anything other than a glowing report? No, so it's a waste of your time and mine (references can be more useful for freelancers and employees—and if you run across someone who can't find three people to say something nice about them, that's a big red flag).

If you haven't worked with an agency before, you're trying to counter your risk and hedge your bet on the most favorable outcome. The biggest thing an agency can do is guarantee their work, though most avoid doing so. Instead, the best-case scenario for both parties might be negotiating mutually agreeable performance-based contracts.

You should also be wary of agencies that are too flexible with price. It may seem like you're getting a great deal, but a good agency understands the costs associated with the work they're proposing to do. They know what they're worth and what the investment should be. When an agency is willing to decrease that amount, they may be unaware of the market needs. They're sacrificing themselves from a quantitative perspective. Remember, you want an agency that knows their value. When hiring an agency—or even a freelancer or employee—you can have two, but not three, of the Iron Triangle: you can have someone who is good and fast, but they're going to be expensive; you can have someone who works fast and cheap, but it won't be very good; or you can have someone who does good, cheap work, but it's going to take a long time.

Look for an agency that specializes as opposed to working in all industries. Having a specialty shows that they understand the benefits of niching and have chosen to become an expert in their area rather than a jack-of-all-trades but master of none.

Finally, do they eat their own dog food—meaning, do they practice what they promise? If you're looking to hire an SEO agency, do they rank for SEO for lawyers? If they can't do their own SEO properly, how can you trust them to do yours?

Because you have less control over the process, establish key performance indicators (KPIs) that are predictive (leading indicators) as well as lagging indicators, quantitative KPIs as a means to show production and activity, and qualitative KPIs that show the number of leads and signed cases (we'll discuss this more in chapter 8).

Congratulations on making it this far! You now have a better idea of how to market and who can help you market—but you're not done yet. Chapter 7 looks at where you'll want to market your firm.

7

TIME TO TAKE ACTION

"The Holy Trinity [of digital marketing] are radio, television, and Google—if you don't have those three things working in concert, your ad campaign is not going to be as effective as it could be."

–MARC ANIDJAR OF ANIDJAR & LEVINE
Personal Injury Mastermind podcast episode 92

HE MAIN PRINCIPLE BEHIND MARKETING IS A SIM-ple one: you need to be *known*. As a personal injury attorney, you are in a saturated market. It's impossible to know when an accident will occur, so you need to be both memorable and easily found. This is different, and especially important, in the personal injury space because you are not soliciting

7

777

7

customers like other advertising businesses do; instead, you are putting your name out there so people will remember who you are and contact you when they need your services.

But you can't just put your name out there once and hope that people remember it when they need you. You have to *keep telling them* who you are and where they can find you. Repetition represents an important part of personal injury marketing, because repetition helps people learn *and retain* who you are. They need to hear you on the radio—or see your billboard or like your social media—enough times for you to become memorable.

If you just do a little advertising here and there, the result is not worth the expense. No one remembers one ad they saw one time, so you'd be better off saving your money and not advertising at all. We are all bombarded with a proliferation of marketing messages all the time, and consumers have become educated to defend against those messages—that's why we don't always click on Google Ads or we mindlessly scroll past Facebook Ads. Often, we don't even realize we're doing it; we've been psychologically programmed to ignore solicitations.

So how *should* you be advertising to ensure people know who you are and how to find you? Hell, where does marketing even take place?

Well, if marketing is all the things that you do to attract prospective clients to your firm—as I established in the introduction—then the different marketing channels are the actions you actually take to reach those clients.

In the rest of the chapter, we'll take a look at different marketing channels—broken into digital, traditional, and grassroots—and how they work better together. I'll give you a TL;DR summary of the impact for each channel and why it can be an important addition to your marketing strategy.

DIGITAL

Digital channels fall into two main categories:

- Search
- Social media

Search

The "search" subset of digital channels consists of Google local service ads, Google Ads, local SEO, organic search, and over-the-top (or OTT) media. Let's take a closer look at each.

Google Local Service Ads

Local service ads are what show up at the very top of a Google search. In terms of virtual real estate, it's "above the fold." This is a pay-per-lead channel, meaning you are charged when the prospective client contacts you via the ad.

Google looks at three performance components of local service ads, which you can think of as the three Rs:

- Region
- Response
- Reviews

Region is the physical location of your office compared to the consumer search. You may not have a lot of control over this aspect as it relates to ranking and gaining position, because your physical, brick-and-mortar location just...is where it is. Some firms have gone remote and no longer operate from offices, but for those that do, it can be cost-prohibitive to move the physical location.

Response refers to your firm's response time in communications: answering phone calls, managing the dashboard, and replying to the messages your consumers send. In general, people in the legal field have a good intake system or backup call center. The variable then becomes: How can you manipulate your response to stand out? If you're already answering the phone, how do you answer more calls? You can expand the categories you advertise in and increase your bids. You can increase response by getting more activity and going after more cases—although, of course, you have to weigh that against your time and the tire kickers that may come from that.

Obtaining more reviews helps you rank better in Google local service ads, among all the Google search advertising options. This relationship can quickly become the age-old riddle of "Which came first, the chicken or the egg?" You have to get more business before you can get more reviews, but you also need more reviews in order to get more business.

When it comes to reviews, you need both quantity and quality. Not only is it important for you to receive reviews in order to rank and for someone to hire you, you also need to have a high review rating in order to rank for superlative queries ("best," "top," "most," "highest," etc.). If you go on vacation and search for "best restaurants near me," you're not going to see one-star restaurants in a population-dense area; you're going to see those with five stars, or 4.9. The same is true when a potential client searches for "best car accident lawyer" or "top truck accident attorney." If you don't have a high review rating, you won't capture superlative queries, which tend to be your best types of cases—when someone types a validating modifier like that, they are looking for maximum compensation.

However, out of all the marketing initiatives we'll look at in this chapter, you have the least control over this one as a personal injury attorney. This aspect can be complemented with other services.

Google Ads

Google Ads is also known as pay-per-click advertising (or PPC), which means that you pay every time someone clicks on your ad, even if they never contact you. There are a few things that can impact your ability to perform in Google pay-per-click. The first is your messaging. You want to have a unique selling proposition

(USP) and target keywords that have consumer intent. (We looked at exactly how to do this in chapters 2 and 3.) You also need a great website that highlights your USP with an excellent landing page to convert the consumer, one that quickly signals trust, as visitors likely don't know you or your firm.

The amount you will spend on Google Ads depends on the needs of your firm. Firms with wide case-selection criteria (ones that will take soft-tissue cases, for example) can achieve very low cost-per-acquisition metrics. But if your requirements are quite strict, then you must be willing to spend more to obtain a client.

Google Ads is often the quickest way to get traffic and visibility compared to other options, because as soon as you pay, you can start gaining visibility. It's also the quickest way to waste money if you don't know what you're doing. There are constantly new extensions and new methods for bid optimization. Having details on your demographics and even psychographics can play a huge factor in how well you'll perform on Google Ads—skip back to chapter 3 if you need a refresher.

Local Search Engine Optimization (SEO)
Local SEO is Google Maps. Ranking in Google Maps is based on three factors:

- Relevance
- Distance
- Prominence

Relevance refers to how related your business is to consumer searches. This includes the words and phrases on your website, as well as those used by individuals when leaving a review or referencing your business.

Distance has the same restriction as Google local service ads, because it's based on proximity. While proximity has decreased over time due to mobile device usage, it still factors into your ranking.

Prominence means being everywhere—and that's what Google wants. To rank in prominence, you're on Google search; you have links, articles, and directories; and you have a high Google review count and score. Again, this rating is important, because if you want to rank for superlatives like "top" and "best," you need a review rating to match. (This review rating is not to be confused with directly saying you're the top attorney or best firm, which, again, is against advertising ethics for attorneys.)

Organic Search

Organic search represents the lion's share of the Google search market because it hits all areas of the funnel, from awareness to investigative to transactional, whereas the other options typically only show up on a transactional query. For example, if someone types in "car accident lawyer," you're definitely going to show up in a Google local service ad and on Maps, but if someone searches "what are the steps I need to take after a car accident," those results are probably not going to show an ad or a Maps entry.

Thousands of variables influence ranking in organic search, but they generally fall into three categories:

- Content
- RankBrain
- Links

You've likely heard the phrase "content is king." In the personal injury space, quality content is table stakes (that is, the bare minimum buy-in to even play the "game"). You *must* have exceptional content, because all of your competitors have car accident and truck accident lawyer landing pages. Yours has to be as good as theirs to even start gaining traction—and needs to be better to surpass them. The words and phrases you want to rank for also have to appear on your website in order to be seen in Google search.

RankBrain is Google's machine-learning algorithm. It looks at behavior like the amount of time an individual spends on your site, the number of pages they visit, and how quickly your website loads. It can also see if a consumer then makes another query after they visit your website and if they go to a different website (which would suggest your site didn't meet their needs). This algorithm is all about tracking how the user interacts with your website to address their intent and their needs—which means *you* need a high-quality website that loads quickly, is easy to navigate, has good information, and is aesthetically pleasing.

The third component is links, which you gain when another website references your URL and refers to your website. If you're trying to win an election, you want to get as many votes as possible; if you're trying to "win" the top results in Google, you want to get as many links as possible. All links are not created equal, however. A link from *The Wall Street Journal* and heavily curated editorials like *Forbes* are significantly better than new blogs or relative unknowns.

Ultimately, you have to have great content, you have to have a good website, and you have to get your content endorsed through links. Most professional writers can produce good content. Many websites are easy to optimize now with all the no-code features, so you don't have to be a developer to make changes. The difficult piece, due to the nature of the industry, is acquiring links. Having relationships and a trusted partner who knows where and how to acquire links is immensely important. (One caveat: Don't take your agency's word for it when they say they're link-building. Make them prove that they are actually building those links through reports and transparency you can see and read. Content links are fairly ethereal, so you need to validate and confirm that those activities are occurring.)

GOAT QUOTE

Matthew Dolman of Dolman Law Group came on episode 25 of the podcast to discuss next-level legal SEO strategies. He has a ton of valuable insight to share:

> By around '16, '17, we became one of the top five personal injury law firms in the country in terms of search volume, and now we're the second-most-searched firm in the country, besides Morgan & Morgan...
>
> I was able to laugh at some of my friends who laughed at me back in the day when they said, "Matt, you're wasting your time with the internet. You're spending so much time; I can't believe you're doing all this. You're putting all your eggs in one basket," which I wouldn't say it's putting in one basket anyway. We have a diverse marketing approach...
>
> At the end of day, content is king. We talked about that over and over again, and the proof's in the pudding. I realized early on that I can't compete with the big boys; at least [back] then I couldn't on TV and radio. And still I couldn't go head to head with Morgan & Morgan, in terms of television ad buys, but what I could compete with them on is Google. You can't really unless you're paying for tons of pay-per-click, which by

the way, more eyeballs go to organic than they do to pay-per-click...But you can't really buy your way into Google. It's a game plan you have to follow. It's a marathon, not a sprint. You can compete with the biggest of the biggest on Google. It's an even playing field... Everyone's looking for that quick fix, maybe pay-per-click. And even that doesn't work that well.

Really, it's SEO, if you're willing to see it through and work on your content, and let Chris [Dreyer] and his team help you with building out the links, building out the content—they do a great job with that as well, on building up the site—within a year, year and a half, you could really be a force to be reckoned with. It's much cheaper than television, radio, billboards, or any other advertising medium you can think of, because you can do it on a very small scale at $10,000, $15,000 a month, where a TV ad buy's gonna cost you $30,000 to $50,000 a month. You really want to play with the big boys probably more than that. Same with radio. Billboards are like a thousand dollars a pop—and that's more of a shotgun advertising that you're hoping that the individual who goes by your billboard needs you at that very time, because otherwise it's just branding. SEO is both branding and it really does generate leads if you're ranking for key terms.

Over-the-Top (OTT) Media Service

Another form of advertising is OTT, or over-the-top media service. This refers to any streaming service that delivers content over the internet. As people move away from traditional TV and cable, they're moving to streaming, which includes Netflix, Hulu, Amazon, Disney+, Apple, Peacock, Max, and a plethora of others. It's a very fractured environment, but there's a huge audience that continues to grow.

As this channel continues to develop, consolidation will occur (it has already started), and advertising options will improve. In 2024, targeting capabilities are very strong from a digital perspective, but your CPM (cost per thousand impressions) is also very high on these channels compared to other options.

Social Media

I'm going to categorize social media as a whole, because while the platforms change and some strategies differ, the general concepts are relatively universal. As of the writing of this book, the top social media networks are Facebook, Instagram, Twitter/X, TikTok, YouTube, and LinkedIn. This will change, as new social communities are always evolving (such as the recently released Threads, Meta's answer to Twitter/X).

Whatever social media you choose to use, you need to contextualize your message to the platform. Content you put on LinkedIn should be business-oriented, whereas Instagram tends to be geared more toward younger millennials and Gen

Z, and Facebook has a more Boomer-based audience. Typically, social media networks give a boost for engagement, because it's a signal to the platform that the content is valuable and therefore should be shown to more users.

Be cognizant of new features, because they typically alter the algorithm to get adoption. Most social media networks follow the same monetization plan: in the beginning, the organic reach from your content will be high because they need to get adoption and more members into the community (Meta's Threads is currently in this phase, as of the writing of this book). For example, when slide decks first came out on Instagram, any post that used the slide deck would show up significantly more on the organic side compared to a standard post with just an image, because Instagram wanted to encourage adoption of the new feature. Over time, however, as a given type of content inventory increases, it becomes pay-to-play. And you have to pay, because your free content doesn't get seen as easily; platforms downgrade the algorithm to incentivize advertising spend.

You also need to focus on both quantity and quality. You need to have enough content and information out there to be known, and you need repetition because your post is only up for a moment before it's gone forever—consumers will rarely visit your historical feed.

Your creative collateral is also immensely important. Typically, social media users don't read the small font as much as they consume images and videos. You can also make your content searchable through tags or hashtags.

Podcasting

Podcasts gained significantly more users during the COVID-19 pandemic. Podcasting can feel more personal and intimate than other channels, because your voice is in the listener's ear. They begin to feel like they know you, especially when they listen frequently. I find it's a great way to build trust and give value without asking for something in return.

My friend Robert Engel says that podcasting is the only channel where you can buy time, because this form of marketing travels with people on their commutes to work and as they go about their days—they typically don't skip ads when listening to podcasts (or the radio), because they're driving. It ends up being forced attention that still works, as opposed to traditional TV advertising, which is dying out as most people move to streaming.

The biggest recommendation I can give for podcasting is to find a style that works for you, whether that's interviewing or a solocast, and stick to a specific cadence, whether daily or weekly (monthly is probably not often enough; I would recommend weekly at a minimum). Like all platforms, including SEO and social, you need an inventory of content. Part of why Joe Rogan got so popular was because he had been doing daily interviews for years, so he had an unmatched inventory of content.

The best ways to grow a podcast are through email marketing, advertising on other podcasts, and using on-platform advertisements—and, of course, having a quality show that people talk about in the first place.

As you know by now, I'm the host of the *Personal Injury Mastermind* podcast. As I grew my podcast following, I found it was obviously beneficial to have interesting guests, because that led to great conversations. That should go without saying, right? However, I also learned that guests sometimes try to get into a loop, where they talk about the same topics they're familiar with across multiple interviews; it's easier for them, since they can fall into a comfortable dialogue without a lot of stress. The downside for me, of course, is that it made it hard for my interviews to stand out. I learned to avoid this loop by doing extensive prep for each guest and asking unique, original questions to spark new and interesting conversations. It can also be helpful to carefully choose the people you have as guests with respect to the theme of your show.

The name of your podcast is important because Apple Podcasts is a search engine of sorts, so if your podcast is more easily searchable, more users can find it. Postproduction is also really important, as is activating your guest so you can piggyback off their audience, email list, and social media platforms.

Email

When people think of marketing, they often focus on prospects and new clients. In reality, there are three phases:

- Prospective clients
- New clients
- Past clients

Email thrives in the third category. It allows past clients to keep you top of mind, which can be crucial for client referrals. If they already had a good experience with you, it's not a bad thing to keep yourself in their field of vision, so to speak.

GOAT QUOTES

In episode 117 of the *Personal Injury Mastermind* podcast, I was able to speak with Brandon Yosha of Yosha Law about innovation and the firm's notable newsletter. Here's what he had to say (with some bonus advice from marketing guru Jay Abraham):

> We send [the newsletter] once a month, and we send it via email. We send a printed version to all of our past and current clients, and people always say, "Hey, I saw the newsletter. I love getting the updates." We try to provide updates on new laws that are being incorporated or results that we had recently got for a past client that might be in a similar situation to a current client. It helps a lot, and they get that newsletter and

then they say, when they go to dinner that night, "Hey, I just got a newsletter from Yosha Law. You were in a car accident, [or] you had a slip and fall. You should call Yosha Law. I just saw that newsletter, and they helped us a long time ago."

It's that top-of-mind awareness. And my cousin is Jay Abraham, who's one of the brightest minds out there when it comes to marketing, and he talks about preeminence and the theory of preeminence and being top of mind all the time, even if it's subconsciously. When you're sending out a newsletter, it's more about the subconscious than it is the conscious, because you want to establish your preeminence and you want people to—whenever that moment comes where they need a lawyer and they've been involved in an act of negligence and they don't know who to trust, they don't know what to do, and the insurance company is treating them like crap—then in that moment, the subconscious mind will connect to Yosha Law. And that's what Jay has taught me.

———————

Dave Abels of Abels & Annes joined me on episode 203 of the podcast to talk about some of the digital channels that his firm uses for steady growth:

Newsletters are critical. It used to be that you could have a fantastic settlement for a client and they might love you, but way back when, once they left, if they lost your card or your number, you wouldn't see them again. Now, with email and newsletters and things like that, you could stay in touch...I'm not someone that has a weekly newsletter...it might be more quarterly. I try to make it where I have a very high percentage of newsletter opens when I send them out because I have something to say. I probably add twenty people to my list for every person that leaves, because I don't bother the heck out of people, but it's enough where they remember you.

But there's other forms of engagement as well. We do our best to have good relationships with our clients. I mean I get, especially after a case settles, I can't tell you how many clients I'm Facebook friends with or friends with on some form of social media, good experiences with our firm, things like your own personal social media...When you have well over a thousand Facebook friends and people know what you do, that tends to bring in some good referrals.

TRADITIONAL

I'm going to say right up front that my specialty is digital marketing. Traditional advertising is not my expertise, so I'm going to lean heavily on some of my podcast guests who are more knowledgeable about this area. That said, we can look at three areas of traditional advertising: television, radio, and outdoor advertising.

Television

In my conversations with Glen Lerner, James Farrin, and Greg Ward, all three said the same thing: you have to saturate the market and be one of the top three spenders in order to stand out in television advertising. Daytime television and sports are effective markets. The demographic tends to be older, but because we're talking about traditional TV and not streaming, it's not as affluent as it used to be—everyone else is spending their money on multiple streaming services.

GOAT QUOTE

Greg Ward says, "There's something I call the tipping point, where if you don't buy a big enough advertising contract, you will not reach a certain saturation and you will not get calls at all. But you cross the tipping point—and it may just

be another 20 or 30 percent—but you cross
the tipping point, then you're actually at critical mass, you can get cases."

If you're advertising on TV, you have to be entertaining and
have a sense of virality. This is Jim Adler charging at a semi-
truck with his sledgehammer or Darryl Isaacs's spoof of Marvel
and *Star Wars*. The virality grabs people's attention and helps
with memorability, which is especially important considering
that we've all become conditioned to ignore attempts to sell to
us. This is also why the Super Bowl is one of the most effective
forms of advertising—not only is there a huge audience, but
everyone wants to watch the commercials too. When else do
people ever *want* to watch advertising?!

Radio

Marc Anidjar calls TV, radio, and digital the Holy Trinity of
advertising—and he should know, considering he's one of the
top radio advertisers.

I've also had the pleasure of talking to Gary Sarner, who is
an expert in radio marketing. He says that, similar to TV advertising, you have to saturate the radio market and run spots that
are close together, for the sake of repetition. When I went to a
National Trial Lawyers summit and took a twenty-minute Uber
ride, I heard Anidjar & Levine's radio spot *four times*! Because I

heard it that many times, I remembered it—whereas if I'd only heard it once, I might not have.

Outdoor Advertising

Billboards and other forms of outdoor advertising (such as vehicle wraps) follow very similar principles to what we've stated across all advertising: stand out and try to go viral.

No one does billboards better than John Morgan of Morgan & Morgan. His "Size matters" billboards lean into the dad humor and innuendo, which causes conversation and virality because it's *just a little* edgy. His billboards are so effective because he plays up the humor, he has enough billboards to saturate the city, the font and copy are easy to absorb, and there's always a clear call to action. There's also enough variance—if you see the exact same billboard every time, you eventually ignore it, but if you see something different occasionally that complements the overall campaign, it's far more effective.

A vanity or repeater phone number can also assist with a billboard's memorability. Mike Morse, for example, has 855-MIKE-WINS. That's the kind of message you want a potential client to retain.

I also have to highlight Alexander Shunnarah. I have no clue how many billboards he has at this point, but it's well over three thousand. His "Call me, Alabama" and "Call me, Boston" campaigns have made him a local celebrity—people even dress up as him for Halloween!

GRASSROOTS

Grassroots marketing can include attending and/or sponsoring networking events and conferences, charitable giving, or just getting out in your community and shaking hands. This is most effective when you have a niche, because you're congregating with people who are like you. (Think of the Law Tigers advertising at Harley-Davidson and motorcycle events to develop relationships with local Harley dealers and riders.) There's something to be said for shaking people's hands and making local appearances that show potential clients you're like them. Because who do people like most? People similar to themselves.

You can also participate in charities and goodwill campaigns (like the backpack or turkey giveaways that you see at back-to-school time or Thanksgiving) to become known in the community. Marketing is all about know, like, and trust. When you give away turkeys, people will know you because you are part of the community, they're going to like you because you're giving away stuff, and they'll trust you because people trust people they know more than people they don't know. Gordon McKernan Injury Attorneys in Louisiana has Gordon Gives, and they're a huge part of the community. The firm gives away bicycles and car seats, sponsors softball teams, and donates to hundreds of organizations.

GOAT QUOTE

When I asked Gordon why giving back is so important to him and his firm on episode 57 of the *Personal Injury Mastermind* podcast, he told me:

> My dad was always a very giving person. You know, he just had a big old heart. His thirst for justice, literally, it was not normal. Cases would come in the door, and he just took them and he ran with them. And they were tough cases, but he always believed in giving voice to things that didn't have it. So I guess I had that in my backdrop. And then I would say that my faith, my Christian faith, just being aware of the privilege and the blessings that I've had and the responsibility, I think, that comes with that. [It's an] "if much is given to you, much is expected" type of attitude. You can't just take from something and not give back to the community at large...There's injustice in the world, and it could be just people need a gift, a helping hand, an organization needs some more funds or needs some people to volunteer for something.

ANOTHER WAY TO LOOK AT MARKETING

Instead of looking at marketing strictly by channel, you can also break it down into paid, owned, and earned media.

Paid media consists of things like TV ads, radio ads, paid social media, Google Ads, or podcast sponsors—any type of ad where you pay someone else to put your promotion in front of more people.

Owned media is anything you functionally own, like the content on your website, your building, your email list, your SEO and content marketing, social media followers, and even things like reviews.

Finally, earned media is something that can't be bought and that you don't necessarily own. It could be getting asked to be a commenter on a media network because of your reputation as an expert, a funny post that goes viral and gets you a bunch of reshares, or having a billboard that really stands out. It's using expertise or entertainment for virality—earning those eyeballs and getting people talking.

GOAT QUOTE

In episode 219 of the *Personal Injury Mastermind* podcast, Daniel Morgan of Morgan & Morgan talks about the firm's "Purple Cow" meetings (named after the Seth Godin concept of showing people something unexpected, which makes them want to tell other people about it), where they brainstorm creative, out-of-the-box ideas to get people talking about them in the media:

> There [are] two different types of earned media too. There's that type of earned media where you get people to talk, and there's the other type that we do a great job of too, which is just PR around big cases…but the stuff you're talking about, my dad calls it "being sticky," getting in people's brains and just sticking there.
>
> We have these sessions every week. People pitch different ideas, and we roundtable it and we kick it around, and then, it's called the Purple Cow meeting, that marketing term when people see something and it sticks with them.

To keep people talking, Morgan & Morgan have even been known to go out and add graffiti to their own billboards—an idea that likely arose from one of their Purple Cow meetings!

Many attorneys fail at earned media. They'll pay for TV or pay-per-click or Facebook Ads, or they'll do organic social, but they don't make it to the point where the media talks about them. As a result, they don't get additional attention and distribution for free.

If you put up a billboard that is similar to everyone else's, you're not creating conversation or any viral effect. But when you use humor or take a controversial approach—that gets talked about.

It's the same for social media. Why are some accounts successful and others aren't? The common factor among social media standouts is earned media. Attorneys are typically not earning the free likes and reshares; they have to pay to get eyeballs on their content. They're not creating organic content that gets engagement.

Earned media is not just about posting a lot of content; you have to capture attention, which typically comes through entertainment. Look at James Helm of TopDog Law: his social media gets a lot of earned media because it's entertaining and appeals to a wide audience, not just the individual who's been in a car accident and needs an attorney.

You can even decrease your direct advertising costs when you use them to go viral, thereby bringing in the earned media.

GOAT QUOTE

In episode 141 of *Personal Injury Mastermind*, Steve Fretzin, host of the *Be That Lawyer* podcast, says:

You're building relationships, you're developing strategic partners, people that refer you business on a regular basis. And then on top of that, you're building the marketing side. Your podcast is building your network of potential buyers and strategic partners. Your social media is on autopilot. You're posting now every day with good content, you're writing a book, and that book is being pushed to bestseller status. Whatever it is, it's all working in your favor and you're either doing something, or you're doing nothing, or you're doing something in the middle—and the people that are doing the most are going to end up in a better position in the future. There's just no way that can't happen.

COMPLEMENTARY MARKETING

Many attorneys look at their approach to channels like a funnel: You get awareness, you find prospective clients, you convert them, and then you're done. At the bottom of the funnel, all the energy is dispelled and it's just...*over*. The end.

Instead, I want you to look at different marketing opportunities as a flywheel, where the more clients you get, the more they power the wheel—and the more you lower the friction of the wheel, the better you can do.

Let's look at the biggest-picture flywheel, not for any channel, but for marketing overall.

You market your firm to acquire clients. You create a good user experience, then ask for a review. You obtain a review, which leads to more referrals—which then lead back to more clients. Whereas in the funnel clients are a means to an end—you get them, you get their money, and you move on—in the flywheel, customers are at the very center. After all, they are *why you are in personal injury law.*

Beyond that foundation, we can use flywheels to demonstrate the capacity for complementary channels to create something bigger than any channel individually. Doing radio alone is good, but pairing radio ads with billboards is better, because it creates and reinforces the repetition that you need. Instead of one plus one equaling two, the continuity will enhance each element, so it's more like one plus one adding up to four. Radio ads and billboards work better together, as do organic SEO and local SEO, podcasting and networking, or grassroots and social media. Some combination of content plus outreach is more effective than just writing content, because people see you in multiple places. They get to know your name and remember you. You build goodwill and interest—developing that "know, like, and trust" factor that is vital for potential clients to choose *you.*

GOAT QUOTE

On the *Tip the Scales* podcast, Amanda Demanda says, "If you don't build a brand, it's going to be hard to originate things just by one medium, like SEO or just Instagram or just TV, because people are expecting you to be a complete company and brand."

Personal injury attorneys should think about some flywheels in particular. The first one would be content marketing with SEO. You create content, optimize its SEO, and perform outreach so people see it and link to it, which in turn helps more people see the next piece of content with improved rankings.

As another example, podcasts offer a method of creating long-form content that you can transcribe into blog content and repurpose for social media. The more podcast episodes you create effectively, the more downloads and subscribers you will get, and the greater your distribution on Apple Podcasts will be. You then acquire more followers on social media, which also increases the distribution, making it more likely other individuals will want to come on your show—thus lowering the friction of obtaining guests.

As you can see, sometimes tactics work together to eliminate friction and power a flywheel that can turn faster and faster.

GOAT QUOTE

In episode 153 of the *Personal Injury Mastermind* podcast, Jordan Ostroff of Jordan Law talks about the flywheel concept:

> The more that you turn [the client] into a referral source, or repeat business, or them coming back to you, then you're saving marketing spend. They know what to expect, they're talking you up well to future clients, having been through the process. I mean, it's just this flywheel. As much as that's, I think, an overplayed term, it really does hit the nail on the head...
>
> We've got this giant oversized wheel, and you push on it, and guess what? Nothing happens. And you keep pushing on it and nothing happens. And you keep pushing on it and then it spins slowly. And you push again and it's faster, and it's faster, and it's faster. The $5,000 case today, that client becomes a referral source for a $5,000 case tomorrow, is now worth ten grand over the lifetime value. And then you can spend that money on more people, and you can spend that money on more ads, and you can spend that money on more content. You have that opportunity to get more clients, to then maximize the value of their cases, and turn them into referral sources. It just builds and builds and builds,

and so suddenly you've got that flywheel spinning, spinning, spinning, and spinning. Even though every push didn't do much, it was just enough to keep it going on its own.

Finally, your target client will determine the best marketing channels for you to use.

If you're marketing to consumers to generate your own cases from them (B2C), the methods you use will differ from those that advertise to other attorneys. You're going to do TV, radio, and social media marketing directed right to your consumer. You'll speak in less legalese, because you're trying to reach people who are not lawyers.

If you're advertising to your peers for referrals (B2B), however, you'll want to niche, speak on stage, join major industry associations and masterminds, highlight your big awards, write a book, and win peer-based awards so your peers know who the best is. You might speak on how to be an effective trial attorney. You'll use legalese and more technical terms and be more granular about your expertise.

In general, the best trial attorneys don't do a ton of traditional marketing. Patrick Salvi acknowledges that his firm doesn't do TV or billboards—but they do have an internal PR team, and they apply to every single award. Joe Fried, the nationwide trucking accident attorney, is not going hardcore on

TV and radio; instead, he's speaking at every conference, meeting his peers, teaching people how to be an effective truck accident attorney, and serving on trucking boards of association for safety. He's a known quantity in that niche and an expert in that area of the law.

On the other hand, I have no idea about anything Glen Lerner has accomplished recently—but when I was in Vegas recently, I saw his billboards at least ten times. Consumers know him. Similarly, John Morgan advertises a ton, and he's the biggest PI attorney in the country. I don't know any specifics about his trials, but I see him on TV all the time and his billboards are everywhere. Why? Because his advertising caters to consumers, not other attorneys.

Most people just focus on the front end of marketing, but you need to consider the entire experience and the impacts it has at both the big-picture and more granular levels. When you combine multiple marketing channels, you create an opportunity not only to reach more prospective clients but also to have those clients remember you—which is, after all, the only way for them to find you when they need a personal injury attorney.

GOAT QUOTE

Jennifer Gore-Cuthbert, founder of Atlanta Personal Injury Law Group, says, "Marketing is not just one thing; it's twenty things. People want to know the magic pill. It's a lot of different things working all at the same time."

Once you've thought more about which channels to use to market your firm, you'll want to pay attention to how well they're performing so that you know what is working and what to change. Chapter 8 will show you how to measure success.

8

MEASURING SUCCESS

"You go to a sporting event and you see a jumbotron, and it's got a bunch of numbers on there; that's a football game. How do you know which players to put on the field? What play to call? If you don't know the score of the game, if you don't know the time left, who's got how many time-outs, what's the down and distance—you just have to have that data in order to make intelligent decisions."

–JOHN NACHAZEL, COO OF MICHAEL MORSE LAW FIRM
Personal Injury Mastermind podcast episode 54

HAVE YOU SEEN THE FAMOUS CHRIS FARLEY MOVIE *Tommy Boy*? There's a scene where Farley's character, Tommy, talks to a potential customer who wants to know why there isn't a guarantee printed on the box.

"Let's think about this for a sec, Ted," Tommy says to him. "Why would somebody put a guarantee on a box? Here's the way I see it, Ted. Guy puts a fancy guarantee on a box because he wants you to feel all warm and toasty inside."

"Yeah," Ted replies, "Makes a man feel good."

"'Course it does. Why shouldn't it? You figure you put that little box under your pillow at night, the Guarantee Fairy might come by and leave a quarter, am I right, Ted?"

They go back and forth for a bit, until Ted finally asks, "But why do they put a guarantee on the box?"

Tommy tells him, "Because they know all they sold ya was a guaranteed piece of shit. That's all it is, isn't it? Hey, if you want me to take a dump in a box and mark it 'guaranteed,' I will. I got spare time. But for now…ya might wanna think about buying a quality product from me."

You may be asking, *What does this have to do with marketing?* Well, marketing doesn't come with guarantees either—which means it's up to you to make sure your marketing efforts aren't getting flushed down the toilet.

PUT ON YOUR LAB COAT AND SAFETY GOGGLES

As we've discussed in previous chapters, marketing is an exercise in attention arbitrage. The game of marketing is to maximize your advertising dollars, spending the least amount of money to get the most impressions. You want to advertise where your prospects congregate, so you have to be willing to adapt and innovate. When something like the metaverse comes along and gets engagement, you want to experiment with that new channel as well. In fact, you need to constantly test and experiment as attention shifts.

If you don't try new things as they come up, you're going to be stuck advertising in the yellow pages or *TV Guide*—once places where everyone's attention could be captured, now quaint relics of long-ago times.

GOAT QUOTE

In episode 242 of the *Personal Injury Mastermind* podcast, Angel Reyes of Reyes Browne Law talks about when he knew it was time to ditch TV ads and go all-in on digital:

> Because we use a unique number for every single ad we do ever, we knew the TV wasn't working. Now I know there's some folks that swear by TV still, and in small markets maybe it still does work. Dallas is the third-largest metro in the country, and I don't think it works here anymore. I'm a big believer that you shouldn't spend any money on TV, that you should spend all your money on digital to start...
>
> I think certainly if you're starting out, you'd be well advised to stick with the digital lane. One, you

can measure it; two, you can control it. If you decided, "I've spent my budget," tomorrow you can stop spending and you just tell them, "Okay, done." And if you need a few weeks to recover from that, then you can kick back off anytime you want. TV doesn't work like that. You['ve] got to prepay thirty days in advance. You never know how many leads you're going to get, but when you start measuring it, I started realizing that certainly for us, our experience was TV leads were too expensive.

Additionally, as more competitors move into a new channel, it gets more expensive to capture the same amount of attention. Again, it's constantly about asking, "Where can I put my money to work, to get the *most* eyeballs for the *lowest* spend?" If you are an early adopter of a new platform or feature, you are likely spending considerably less to capture incoming attention than people who arrive late to the game.

But that doesn't necessarily mean jumping in with both feet before you know how well a platform will take off. On episode 1 of *The Game Changing Attorney* podcast, John Morgan, the biggest personal injury attorney in the US, says:

The way I calculate risk is the concept of bullets before bombs. Before I go in and do something, I go in with bullets to see if it works. I don't go in with a bomb. Why would I go in with a bomb? I start running some mesothelioma ads on CNN, and if it works, I do some more bullets on MSNBC, and then I do bullets on Fox…and then all of a sudden, I let the bombs out. So my risks are calculated risks, and it's bullets before bombs. Once I know the bullets are working, once I know what I'm doing is working, then and only then do I unleash [the bombs]. A lot of people make a huge mistake by going in before they're ready.

Measuring success is all about experimenting and testing. These are the bullets John talks about: a test run to see if a new ad, platform, or marketing channel works for you *before* deciding to commit considerable marketing resources toward it. Because you never know exactly what's going to catch fire, you have to experiment with different aspects—whether that's different content or a different social media strategy.

But in order to determine the results of your tests and experiments, you need to analyze data. That means you need to set up tracking and attribution. In the PI space, some of the most basic tracking would be phone numbers (CallRail is the current technology most people use to track calls) and goal conversions on a website, typically through Google Analytics. You can track some of these metrics through direct integrations with your CRM.

From there, you need to establish benchmarks—how many cases you're currently getting—so you have a point of comparison.

If you're trying a new channel, and thus don't have any previous points of comparison, you need to run an initial pilot to get data.

How do you calculate where you need more data or have enough of a dataset? If your fees average $10,000, how much should you put into paid social to determine whether or not it works? Is it a dollar amount? A number of impressions? A number of contacts? In chapter 1, we established that a percentage of your budget should go toward marketing, but now we're breaking it down further. How much of that budget should go toward which areas of marketing—and when are you getting diminishing returns and, thus, should pull back? (Most CRMs will give you data to help with these decisions.)

GOAT QUOTE

In episode 227 of the *Personal Injury Mastermind* podcast, James Helm of TopDog Law says, "Once you've really gotten clear about your data—on what does it cost to acquire a client, how long is the duration that they're on your desk, and what's that fall-off percentage—you can start to look at your average fee and say, 'Oh, I can get this aggressive trying to spend money to acquire new customers, and I can do it profitably.'"

As much as people want to split-test and do conversion rate optimization (CRO), you need to have enough data to make an informed decision. Let's say someone runs a Google Ads campaign for $10,000 but doesn't get a single call as a result—is it even working? Well, just because they didn't get a call for the first $10,000 doesn't necessarily mean the channel is broken. They may have been undercapitalized for that specific marketing initiative.

So, when you're trying something new, how long or how far do you go before you know whether or not it's working? The answer to this question depends on the channel. SEO, for example, won't give you answers in a month—or even in six months. In my opinion, SEO should be a year-long investment.

Direct response typically has a shorter window. You don't need to run Google Ads for a whole year to see if they work; you might see the results in a month or a quarter with a sufficient sample size.

Branding initiatives like TV, on the other hand, have more of a long-term orientation. You're looking at a much wider dataset to see how a consumer is influenced and how their behavior has changed. Branding creates demand, whereas direct response captures existing demand.

Analyzing your branding also comes into play. In an interview with Ed Herman of Brown & Crouppen, I asked him how to measure the success of a brand campaign. Here's Ed's answer:

You['ve] got to think about what the goal of each type of marketing is. If people sit there and believe that the goal of marketing is solely the end results—how many cases did you get from it? If that's what people were using as the only measure, first of all, it's almost impossible to do a complete attribution of that. But if that were really the case, nobody would ever do something like a billboard. If you were just looking at how many of your clients or customers said, "I signed up with you because I saw your billboard," it would never justify its expense.

And yet, if you were to, instead of measuring billboards by how many cases you got, you measure it by how many of your clients were familiar with your billboards? How many of them had been exposed to your billboards? Were aware of your billboards? It's an awareness play. It's this whole idea of a person needs to be touched by you a certain number of times before you're kind of cemented into the top of their mind.

We just had some brand research done, and when they're doing brand research, they'll do something called "unaided recall," and then they'll do something called "aided recall." Unaided recall would be something like this: they ask a group of people, say, from St. Louis or Kansas City, without any prompting, they'll say, "Make a list of all of the law firms that you can think of off the top of your head." Okay. That's unaided recall. And you know, some of them will write down Brown & Crouppen. I can tell you that 100 percent of them in four different focus groups...wrote down Brown & Crouppen. And aided recall is when they'll give you a list of firms and they'll say, "Mark off whichever of these firms you've ever heard of." And obviously if we're 100 percent unaided, we're 100 percent aided, but you could also see our competition, their name is not right on the top of your head, but if you prompt them and say, "Well, have you ever heard of so-and-so?" that's all, "Yeah, yeah, yeah. I've heard of so-and-so." And those are the kinds of things you have to do to measure the effectiveness of your branding campaigns.

With this process, you can determine how well-recognized your brand is versus your competitors.

MEASURE WHAT MATTERS

There are certain key performance indicators (KPIs) you should track for your marketing. These can be broken up by types of marketing. For direct response, you're going to look at your return on advertising spend. For branding, the core KPIs to be aware of are cost per lead (CPL), cost per acquisition (CPA), and client lifetime value (CLV).

CPL would be your total marketing spend divided by the number of new leads you receive. To calculate CPA, divide the total amount you spend in marketing and sales by the total number of cases you sign. CLV is not just the amount a client's case brings in, but also the amount from any referrals or their evangelism on social media.

You can see that measuring ROI for direct response is cleaner and attribution is easier to see. There are direct relationships, and it's just math: How much did you spend, and how much did you get in return? You're also reviewing information in a shorter window. Branding, on the other hand, is more difficult to quantify, and you have to look at your total marketing costs in order to calculate CPL, CPA, and CLV. But when you know what a client is worth, you know what you can pay to acquire the client.

I find that when you have owned assets *and* a brand *and* memorability, your CPAs are lower. You could advertise in the same TV market as a competitor, for example, but if your commercial has some earned component to it, you can get lower CPAs than someone showing something more generic and less memorable. You get more attention—and therefore more leads and more/better cases. When you're more memorable and you have the brand to back up the earned media, people are more willing to share or talk about your business—and that virality is all free advertising.

GOAT QUOTE

In episode 75 of the *Personal Injury Mastermind* podcast, James Farrin talks about tracking velocity, which most attorneys don't track—and why that's a mistake:

I'm a big believer in analyzing the fees per month. A lot of times lawyers will look at, on a particular case, how much the fee was going to be, which is a very important measure. You want to compare your marketing costs versus your revenue. That return on investment is an important analysis, but I like to go a little farther and also figure out how long it took to get that result. So if I can get a $2,000 fee in six months, that may be better than a $3,000 fee in twelve months, especially if I'm able to replace that $2,000 fee with another one after six months. It's not just the amount of the fee, but it's the velocity that I like to measure. So, I look for practice areas where our fee per month dips below a certain level, and I think, well, those are cases that are not worth taking on anymore.

How Did You Hear about Us?

Another good thing to track is the marketing sources that lead your clients and prospective clients to you. That means having a "How did you hear about us?" field on your forms, so your clients can tell you exactly which channel helped them find you.

Some people recommend having an open text field for leads to write in their answers. Others recommend a drop-down box with a selection of answers for them to choose from. Both approaches have their limitations. If you give people too many options, they get information overload. As a result, they'll just check the first or last option, or some random one—often "Google" or "colleague"—and you won't have complete or correct information. Additionally, there may be multiple attribution points. Even though they selected "Google," they may have also seen your billboard or heard your radio ad.

I had a great conversation with John Berry of Berry Law about this issue on my podcast:

> **John Berry:** [For] our intake or sales team, the first question is always "Who referred you to us?" Because inevitably what happens is we get, "Well, I found you on Google." That was the response.
>
> Then I talk to them, I said, "What do you mean you found us on Google?"
>
> "Well, I went to Google."
>
> "Well, how did you know to look for us?"
>
> "Oh, my dad told me to go find you guys and give you a call."
>
> I said, "Well, that's a referral."
>
> Now I got to train our sales team on what's a referral, I got to train our lawyers on what's a referral, but we have to ask that question "Who referred you to us?" as opposed to just sitting back and hoping that the attribution is right, because that is the scariest part of marketing. You're

spending money everywhere, and usually there's things you can do [so] that...all the ships rise as you spend more money.

Look, when you start out, I would say when you're under $1 million for a firm, you want to do as much direct-response marketing as you can. If you can track the SEO, if you can track the PPC, if you can track your newsletter or whatever you're sending out, do that. But then once you get to eight figures, once you get above $10 million, you're playing the branding game. It's a scarier game because you can't figure out where all that money's going. All you see is that lift. All of a sudden, you're doing the branding, the TV commercials, the billboard, the radio. It's going up, and it may still be coming through the PPC channel, or it may still be coming through SEO, but how do they know to look for your firm? We find now that we spend a lot more money on branding, that our advertiser dollars in branding translate to Google searches of Berry Law.

Chris Dreyer: It does have that rising tides effect. If you're going to do SEO, you got the branded searches, people are going to click on your results more and maybe click on your Google Ads more. It all has this multiplying impact. I've heard Chris Walker talk about, hey, put on your form "How did you hear about us?" Just let them type it in. Sometimes they'll tell a story. Over time, you get to see trends. You get to uncover more information. I think that's

[like] your "Who referred us to you?" Then you're going to get that same type of information. It's like a similar tactic, but very powerful.

John Berry: I got great respect for Chris Walker, the things he's done, [but] I wholeheartedly disagree. When you do that free text, it's not as searchable. It's a lot more work than if you have a drop-down menu. I think it's easier when you give the drop-down, the choices. I don't like the free text anymore, just because I've learned the importance of having good, structured data, and that has really been a game changer. We've lost a lot of opportunities because we did too much free-form on our intake software.

The solution is to have a hybrid of both self-reported and structured attributions with your CRM. You need enough concrete data to make decisions, but you don't want to restrict your clients' choices in telling you how they found you. If you make your survey too limited, you'll never hear that story about how someone talked to someone else's grandma or saw a fridge magnet or saw someone wearing a Berry Law T-shirt at Six Flags and decided to give them a call. The way consumers make decisions has changed—they now go to multiple sources before deciding. You don't want to misattribute something by having an overly narrow selection process.

By allowing clients to write a custom response, you give them the opportunity to communicate those multiple attribution points. When you file it into your CRM, however, you want good, clean, structured data, so you can then select the closest appropriate answer. This allows you to aggregate the data, to measure attribution—and to determine information about how clients *think* they found you.

CONCLUSION

"Let me say as forcefully as I can, advertising works. To understand that, you just have to look around your own communities and look at the lawyers who have done it so effectively for so many years. You just have to look at the advertising budgets of all the companies that trade in the New York Stock Exchange to understand that not only is advertising working, it's essential."

–JOHN MORGAN, *YOU CAN'T TEACH HUNGRY*

Wayne Gretzky is the best player the NHL has ever seen. We can debate whether that GOAT title goes to Michael Jordan or LeBron James in the NBA. But in the PI space, the GOAT of marketing is unequivocally John Morgan.

There's no comparison: He has the largest firm in the country, *by far*—three to four times larger than the second-biggest firm.

They try more cases than any other and, as of 2023, have settled over $15 billion in cases. They've made a massive investment in technology, and they are *everywhere*—with more than nine hundred attorneys, they have locations in every state.

> Note: *Morgan & Morgan is not a client—and we're not trying to get them to become one. I'm highlighting them because there's a good reason they're so big: they do everything you should be doing to* stand out.

Most importantly, however—and most relevant here—Morgan & Morgan, headed by John Morgan, has absolutely nailed paid, owned, and earned media. His positioning is "Size matters," which is fitting for the largest PI firm in America, and it's just a clever use of double entendre. He also has positioning around being "for the people," which his targeting supports. As he says in his book *You Can't Teach Hungry,* "I believe very strongly that before you advertise you need to have a branding statement that will be with you for the rest of your career. I end every ad that I run with the slogan 'For the people.'"

In terms of geographics, he's a nationwide firm, his billboards feature men and women from different ethnicities, and he appeals to a Spanish-speaking demographic.

His messaging is humorous and memorable—one billboard, for example, shows John in a baseball uniform and reads, "We'll go to bat for you." Another has him with his shirt off and highlights "a cool $15 billion dollars recovered." To reach the segment of his demographic that watches UFC, the firm has billboards for the fights, which say, "Fighting is in our DNA."

He knows billboards are a strong marketing channel, a point he highlights in *You Can't Teach Hungry*: "I'm a great proponent of billboards. That gives you top-of-mind awareness and, over time, becomes ingrained in the minds of the people in your city. Billboards are for long-term thinkers."

But he's not only doing billboards; John Morgan utilizes every channel—digital, traditional, and grassroots. He's the king of SEO, he's doing Google Ads and LSA, and Morgan & Morgan has *fifty-five thousand* Google reviews—John refers to Morgan & Morgan as "the Google law firm." They have segmented landing pages throughout their website, as well as abundant Google Business profiles.

Look, I wrote a book on niching, so I clearly believe in its power—and so does John Morgan. His niche is personal injury, and he has people who specialize in all the subsets of that niche so that he can market across all of them. As he puts it on his website, "Our attorneys are solely focused on a specific area of law, whereas other law firms act as a jack-of-all-trades. Our team is large and diverse, but our mission is singular: To deliver the best results for you and your family. Because when you hire

PERSONAL INJURY LAWYER MARKETING

us, we think about you, but we also think about all those who count on you."

John is on all the social media platforms, and his posts go viral all the time. His social media is humorous and entertaining—but he's not just talking about law. He once posted a video about how bad Arby's food was, and Arby's sent him a meat suit (and food) by helicopter to his home in Maui (because there isn't a location in Hawaii)! At Thanksgiving, he posted a big secret: that turkey tastes like shit. And his posts all have tons of comments. Agree with him or not, like him or not—he draws engagement.

He's also on TV and podcasts all the time. He does a ton of grassroots marketing too, particularly with the Morgan & Morgan, P.A. Hunger Relief Center and his For The People Scholarship for students looking to start a law career.

If you look at leverage, he's got it all: in terms of people, with nine hundred attorneys, he has the biggest team; in terms of capital, he's investing the most marketing dollars ($150 million a year!); he's using every major distribution outlet—TV, radio, billboards; and he's leveraging technology as the owner of Litify CRM. From May 2023 to April 2024, he spent over $201 million on advertising, according to Vivvix. Additionally, on his website he says, "We invest millions in our technology and have thousands of employees, a state-of-the-art intake center, mobile reps, unrivaled infrastructure and technology, engineers, investigators, researchers, and scientists."

His branding and messaging are excellent. He has no filter—so he's on TV because he's funny, and he's invited on tons of podcasts because he's entertaining. His confidence shines through. He's the example of testing, with his "bullets before bombs" concept.

Any way you look at it, using any metrics, John Morgan is *the* GOAT.

GOAT QUOTE

There's a lot of wisdom in what John says himself, so I also want to include some of his best quotes.

On episode 1 of *The Game Changing Attorney Podcast* with Michael Mogill, John says:

> "I don't think anybody could wipe me out. I don't think anybody works harder than me. I don't think anybody has the imagination that I have. Look, there was never anybody on the back of phone books, until me. Before I went to law school, I sold yellow pages and I thought, you know, that'd be the place I'd rather be because that's a fifty-fifty chance of just being found right there. There were no lawyers on billboards until me. There were no lawyers on buses until me. I don't think anybody could ever put me out of business. The only

person that could put me out of business would be me. I believe that I'm the greatest legal marketer in the history of legal marketing. We're going to do almost a billion dollars in fees this year. We spent $150 million in advertising. So to totally put me out of business would be hard. Only I could hurt myself."

"It was a way of thinking I used when I was growing out of Orlando. I call it the teacup. I got a teacup, and I am pouring water into the teacup. Once the water starts pouring over the teacup and we get to diminishing returns, I can't grow this business anymore. In Orlando I'd kind of plateaued, then I would move to the next city."

"In the jungle today, a lion will be born. And that lion is the king of the jungle, just because he or she is a lion. The same day, a sloth will be born. Same day, same jungle, same deal. That sloth is so fucked. He can't even describe it. All he can do is barely muster up enough energy to come down the tree, grab some berries, go to the bathroom, and go back up and go to sleep."

In his interview with Luke Russell on the *Lawful Good* podcast (season 1, episode 14), John says:

"There's a seminar out there, a three-hour seminar with CLE credits, is called 'What to Do When Morgan & Morgan Enters Your City'...And I'm like, this the same way you should do before Morgan & Morgan entered your city, which is work your fucking ass off every day. The greatest way to compete with me, is work your fucking ass off."

"Every day you get to win or lose, every single day. And so I do have a lot of competition everywhere I go. And it's not just weak competition. It's strong competition. It's very, very, very smart and capable people. But the way I look at competition is, it makes me better, because I'm competing. If you're running a race, by yourself, a hundred-yard dash and on your mark, get set, go, run one hundred yards. Now, if we run the same race, except we put a wolf behind me, and give me a forty-yard head start, I will promise you I will run faster with the wolf chasing me. So I'm okay with wolves chasing me, because wolves make me go faster."

"I got into this [business] when nobody advertised... But I did it when the people who could wouldn't. So I just advertised when nobody was advertising. And all of a sudden, I got this advantage. Not because I did anything special, just because I was willing to do it. I was willing to take the shit to advertise. Back in the '80s, if you advertised you were just–oh my God. But that gave me an advantage, because I did it when people wouldn't."

"We are absolutely focused on what's in the best interest of our client, rather than what's in our financial best interest. The ultimate question for me is what's best for the client. Because I also believe what's ever best for the client, is also going to be best for me financially. And I'll give you example. At one point in time, I decided to get into mesothelioma business. Now, I'm very good at getting cases. But I got the meso cases, and I had put a group of lawyers together who I ultimately determined were weak. But I knew there were other people doing meso that were very strong. And so one day I said, 'You know what, I'm not doing our clients a favor by handling these cases.' So I made a decision to refer the cases all out, try to place a lot of my people with the firms that I was sending the cases to. And to this day, I refer my mesothelioma cases out to law firms who are really, really good at it. My clients win. And the truth is, I win, because I believe that my referral fees are greater than what regular legal fees would have been. Plus, I have no overhead. The client wins, the referring lawyers that I've referred to win, and I win. And when everybody wins, that's a good deal."

"I've lived my life under this motto. It may be even what I would put on my tombstone, which goes like this: *Nothing is about today. Everything is about tomorrow.* I don't believe you should ever be looking for anything in return. And I believe when you do that, you get everything."

ARE YOU THE GOAT?

What does GOAT marketing mean? To be the GOAT is to be the best-known firm in your market. Let's revisit the definition of marketing from chapter 1: *the process of attracting prospective clients to your firm.*

So, let's see if you are the GOAT of marketing, based on everything you've learned in this book.

Rate yourself. Go through all the questions for each chapter and rate your firm's performance on a scale from one to five— one meaning you haven't even thought about it, five meaning you have that strategy in place and working well.

Questions	Score					Relevant Podcast Episodes
Chapter 1. Types of Marketing						
Do you have a balance of direct response and branding strategies in place to support your firm's goals?	1	2	3	4	5	
Are you using economies of scale to get the most benefit from your marketing strategies?	1	2	3	4	5	
Do you have a strategy for obtaining client referrals?	1	2	3	4	5	• Episode 4, "Using Emotional Intelligence to Boost Your Firm and Client Experience," with Larry Nussbaum of Nussbaum Law Group • Episode 106, "Rethinking Referrals to Help You Scale," with Luis Scott, formerly of Bader Scott Injury Lawyers
Do you have a strategy for obtaining peer referrals?	1	2	3	4	5	
Are you investing a minimum of 20 percent into your marketing efforts?	1	2	3	4	5	• Episode 134, "The Hammer: Insights from a Marketing Legend," with Darryl Isaacs of Isaacs & Isaacs

Chapter 2. Positioning					
Do you have a niche?	1	2	3	4	5

- Episode 63, "How to Become an Expert and Revolutionize Your PI Niche," with Joe Fried of Fried Goldberg
- Episode 235, "Cracking the Code: Specialized Firms Driving Complex Litigation at Scale," with Dawn Smith of Smith Clinesmith
- Episode 238, "Vertical Marketing: Explosive Growth, One Niche at a Time," with Corey Quinn
- Episode 250, "Thrive in Disruption: Future-Proofing Your PI Practice," with Steven Gursten of Michigan Auto Law
- *Bonus*: Episode 82, "The Universal Power of Niche," with Dave Thomas of Law Tigers

Is your firm's marketing entertaining and memorable?	1	2	3	4	5

- Episode 227, "Unreasonable Success: Explosive Growth in Under Five Years," with James Helm of TopDog Law

Question	1	2	3	4	5	Related Episodes
Do you highlight your demographics, experience, winning, and/or value?	1	2	3	4	5	• Episode 116, "Breaking into the Bilingual Market," with Liel Levy of Nanato Media • Bonus: Episode 80, "Doing Well by Doing Good," with Mike Papantonio of Levin Papantonio
Do you stand out?	1	2	3	4	5	• Episode 83, "Differentiation: How to Make Your Law Firm a Purple Cow," with Seth Godin of Akimbo
Do you have a unique selling proposition that highlights how you are different from every other firm?	1	2	3	4	5	• Episode 126, "Crushing a Rebrand: Seamless Intake, Authentic Social, and Core Value Guidance," with Brett Sachs of MVP Accident Attorneys

Chapter 3. Targeting

Question	1	2	3	4	5	Related Episodes
Do you have an ideal customer avatar (or avatars)?	1	2	3	4	5	• Episode 153, "Automation and Marketing: Developing a Personalized Experience," with Jordan Ostroff of Jordan Law
Do you know your avatar's demographics?	1	2	3	4	5	
Do you know their geographics?	1	2	3	4	5	

	1	2	3	4	5	
Are you clear on your avatar's psychographics?	1	2	3	4	5	
Does your marketing speak to your audience, where they are?	1	2	3	4	5	

Chapter 4. Messaging

	1	2	3	4	5	
Does your billboard say any version of "INJURED?" (1), or have you developed a unique, memorable tagline (5)?	1	2	3	4	5	• BONUS: Episode 113, "Building Legacy from Bootstraps: 26 Years of Marketing Innovation," Kyle Bachus of Bachus & Schanker
Is your messaging easy to consume, and does it appeal to a broad audience?	1	2	3	4	5	
Do you show your audience that you are likable, humble and/or self-deprecating, approachable, and trustworthy?	1	2	3	4	5	• Episode 14, "Building a Loveable Brand and Lessons from the Viral Marketing Master," with Ed Herman of Brown & Crouppen • Episode 162, "SEO Updates: What Every Firm Owner Needs to Know," with Matthew Dolman of Dolman Law Group

Do you have a bottom-of-the-funnel ask that specifically targets your avatar?

1 2 3 4 5

Do you utilize the psychology of persuasion to help your prospective clients see why they should hire your firm?

1 2 3 4 5

Chapter 5. Leverage

Do you have a strategy you can leverage for maximum advantage over your competition?

1 2 3 4 5

Are you leveraging labor?

1 2 3 4 5

- Episode 219, "Explosive Growth: Inside the Nation's Leading Personal Injury Firm," with Daniel Morgan of Morgan & Morgan
- Episode 52, "Hiring for Excellence, Interview Strategy, and the New PIP," with Chris Mursau of Topgrading, Inc.

Are you leveraging capital?

1   2   3   4   5

- Episode 209, "Purpose and Profit: Roadmap for Strategic Growth," with Jack Zinda of Zinda Law Group
- Episode 84, "A Steady Hand in a Shifting Industry," with Glen Lerner of Lerner and Rowe
- Episode 122, "Financial Security: How to Build Long-Term Wealth," with Andrew Finkelstein of Finkelstein and Partners
- BONUS: Episode 128, "Be Your Own Bank: How to Fund Your Vision of the Future," with Mark Kull of Capitalis Planning Partners

Are you leveraging technology?

1   2   3   4   5

- Episode 2, "Utilizing Chatbots and AI for Law Firms," with Jessie Hoerman of SimplyConvert
- Episode 13, "Streamlining Practice Management and Revolutionizing Efficiency," with Terry Dohrmann of Litify
- Episode 99, "Collaboration before Competition," with Bob Simon of the Simon Law Group and Justice HQ

Are you leveraging technology? *(continued)*

- Episode 101, "Discovering the Power of Automation," with Pratik Shah of EsquireTek
- Episode 120, "Innovation and Disruption: How Tech Is Driving the Legal Industry Forward," with Anthony Johnson of the Johnson Firm
- Episode 121, "Building Blocks: Create a Virtual, Automated, and Scalable Law Firm," with Sam Mollaei of Legal Funnel
- Episode 138, "How to Win More Cases: Technology in the Courtroom," with Kyle Newman of James Newman, P.C.
- Episode 239, "Toolkit: Legal Tech, Streamline Legal Marketing, Intake, and Operations," with Jack Newton of Clio

1 2 3 4 5

Are you leveraging content?

- Episode 92, "The Secret Sauce for Managing and Marketing," with Marc Anidjar of Anidjar & Levine
- Episode 129, "Podcasting for Attorneys: A Crash Course," with Robert Ingalls of LawPods
- Episode 144, "Omnichannel Marketing: Vision, Execution, and Growth," with Neama Rahmani of West Coast Trial Lawyers

					• Episode 149, "Branded Rideshare Vehicles: Retarget to Quality Leads," with Greg Star of Carvertise

Chapter 6. **Who to Hire**

	1	2	3	4	5	
Have you decided who will perform your firm's advertising?	1	2	3	4	5	
Have you weighed in-house vs. outsourcing?	1	2	3	4	5	• Episode 237, "Capture More Cases: Market Smarter, Partner Stronger," with Bill Pintas of Pintas & Mullins

Chapter 7. **Marketing Channels**

	1	2	3	4	5	
Are you utilizing digital marketing channels?	1	2	3	4	5	• Episode 25, "Legal SEO Strategies to Take Your Firm to the Next Level!" with Matthew Dolman of Dolman Law Group • Episode 117, "Innovation: The New Guard on Foundation and Future Marketing," with Brandon Yosha of Yosha Law • Episode 203, "Steady Growth: Adaptability and Client Services," with Dave Abels of Abels & Annes

Do you perform traditional marketing?	1	2	3	4	5

- Episode 170, "Tactical Growth: Market Saturation and Milestone Hires," with Greg Ward of Ward Law Group

What grassroots marketing do you do?	1	2	3	4	5

- Episode 57, "Law Firm Family Succession and Giving Back," with Gordon McKernan of Gordon McKernan Injury Attorneys

Are you using humor, conversation, and virality to get earned media?	1	2	3	4	5

- Episode 141, "Business Development: How Soft Skills Double Revenue," with Steve Fretzin of the Be That Lawyer podcast
- Episode 219, "Explosive Growth: Inside the Nation's Leading Personal Injury Firm," with Daniel Morgan of Morgan & Morgan

Do you have complementary marketing channels working together for greater effect?	1	2	3	4	5

- Episode 133, "Hyper-growth: Brand Building and Digital Assets," with Jennifer Gore-Cuthbert of Atlanta Personal Injury Law Group
- Episode 153, "Automation and Marketing: Developing a Personalized Experience," with Jordan Ostroff of Jordan Law

Chapter 8. Measuring Success

	1	2	3	4	5	
Are you experimenting with different channels and strategies?	1	2	3	4	5	• Episode 242, "$1B and Counting: Managing and Marketing an Auto Empire," with Angel Reyes of Reyes Browne Law
Are you testing the effectiveness of your current marketing strategies?	1	2	3	4	5	• Episode 227, "Unreasonable Success: Explosive Growth in Under Five Years," with James Helm of TopDog Law
What is your return on advertising spend for your direct-response campaigns?	1	2	3	4	5	• Episode 75, "Efficiency as a Calling Card and Getting Tech to Work for You," with James Farrin of the Law Offices of James Scott Farrin
What are your core KPIs (CPL, CPA, CLV) for your branding initiatives?	1	2	3	4	5	• Episode 14, "Building a Loveable Brand and Lessons from the Viral Marketing Master," with Ed Herman of Brown & Crouppen
Are you tracking how your clients initially found you?	1	2	3	4	5	• Episode 161, "Warrior Ethos: Know Who You Serve, Market Accordingly," with John Berry of Berry Law

Add up your points:

- If you scored from 130 to 144, you can consider yourself a good marketer.
- If you scored from 145 to 164, you can call yourself a *great* marketer.
- But only if you scored 165 or higher can you consider calling yourself the GOAT of marketing in your city.

If you're not the GOAT yet, don't get discouraged: most attorneys aren't, obviously. Look at where your firm has deficiencies, reread those sections of the book or listen to some of the relevant podcast episodes, and improve those areas.

There can only be one GOAT...so why not be that GOAT in your market?

ABOUT THE AUTHOR

Chris Dreyer is the CEO and Founder of Rankings.io, an SEO agency that helps elite personal injury law firms land serious injury and auto accident cases with digital marketing. His company has the distinction of making the Inc. 5000 list six years in a row.

Chris's journey in legal marketing has been a saga, to say the least. A world-ranked collectible card game player in his youth, Chris began his "grown-up" career with a history education degree and landed a job out of college as a detention room supervisor. The surplus of free time in that job allowed him to develop a side hustle in affiliate marketing, where (at his apex) he managed over one hundred affiliate sites simultaneously, allowing him to turn his side gig into a full-time one. When his time in affiliate marketing came to an end, he segued into SEO for attorneys, while also having time to become a top-ranked online poker player.

In addition to owning and operating Rankings.io, Chris is a real estate investor and podcast host, as well as a member of the Forbes Agency Council, the Rolling Stone Culture Council, Business Journals Leadership Trust, Fast Company Executive Board, and Newsweek Expert Forum.

If you're interested in being a guest on the *Personal Injury Mastermind* podcast, email Chris at chris@rankings.io.

www.ingramcontent.com/pod-product-compliance
Lightning Source LLC
Chambersburg PA
CBHW031850200326
41597CB00012B/353